Farmers of Light

Do You Have Ears?

by

James R. Ristau

DORRANCE
PUBLISHING CO
EST. 1920
PITTSBURGH, PENNSYLVANIA 15238

Dorrance Publishing Co
585 Alpha Drive
Pittsburgh, PA 15238
Visit our website at www.dorrancebookstore.com

ISBN: 979-8-88812-354-6
eISBN: 979-8-88812-854-1

Foreword

RJ's Wisdom – Thanksgiving 1986

Think about the richness of our land. The top six inches of our soil are like none found any other place on earth. For long before the prairie was settled, the land abounded with wildlife and waterfowl with no help from man and provided what they needed. This land has provided a livelihood for our grandparents and parents for over a hundred years and will provide for generations to come if we don't ruin it with chemicals and pollution. The whole idea of farming the land is dependent on one miracle of God after another—Consider the birth of young animals, which is left to nature to occur in the spring. The germination of our seed when it is planted, the right amount of moisture soil temperature and sunlight to make things grow. The oxygen the plants produce for us to stay alive. Do these things just happen because of something we do? We who are farmers, more than anyone else, should realize that God is in control and will provide us with what we need. What he asks us to do is "Seek ye first the Kingdom of God"—and the promise—"and all these things will be added unto to you." I thank God that I live in a beautiful land. – R.J. Ristau (1932–2019)

Thanks, Dad.

Forward for Farmers of Light by James Ristau

By Gabe Brown

I first started down the "regenerative" path after a series of natural disasters had decimated my crops for four years in a row. Three years of hail and a year of drought had left me deep in debt with little chance of being able to continue to farm.

I distinctly remember kneeling in one of my pastures and praying to God. I prayed, "God, if you will help see me through this, I will spend the rest of my life helping others to make earth a Kingdom of God."

As I walked back to my pickup, I remember observing things that I had not before; the sweet scent of clover on the summers breeze, the gentle murmur of the rustling leaves of a cottonwood tree, a beetle scurrying ahead of my feet, the "turkey feet" of a big bluestem plant. All things that, no doubt, I had walked by or heard a hundred times before but I had not NOTICED them.

I thought of quote that I heard rancher Don Campbell say a year earlier, "If you want to make small changes, change the way you do things; but if you want to make major changes, change the way you SEE things."

It was then that I realized that if I was to be able to continue to farm it would be by the Grace of God. I needed to work with his creation and not against it. That would require changing the way I SEE things by allowing God's grace to dictate the way I farmed.

I became an Observer of God's creation. As Jim describes in this book, "the job of a Christian farmer is to receive God's grace, through light, to grow and care for his kingdom – and help to bring in His harvest."

Once I opened my life to God's grace and changed the way I saw things, looking at them from his perspective, my farm flourished, my family flourished and my faith flourished.

Jim says it best in this book, "Carbon is an indicator of soil health. Faith is an indicator of soul health."

I encourage you to read this book with an open mind and learn the lessons that Jim shares. Accept God's grace. Together, we can, and will, make earth a kingdom of God.

"And God saw every thing that He had created, and behold, it was very good...
. And the Lord God planted a garden eastward in Eden... and there He put the man, who He had formed...
*And the Lord God took the man, and put him into the garden of Eden **to dress it and to keep it.**"*
Gen. 1:31, 2:8, 2:15 KJV

1

Creation

[1] In the beginning God created the heavens and the earth. Genesis 1

Do you believe this statement? If not, what do you believe? Is this just some metaphorical story written by a crazy society from long ago that was just trying to make sense of things they could not explain? Has science fully debunked this idea and relegated it to merely fairy-tale status? Logically then, if the above statement is not true, then none of the Bible is true, and it can be fully rejected. If this is your belief, that everything can be explained with logic and science, and there is no more to say about it, then you may find the biblical references in this book to be a bit rhetorical. The whole point of this book is to illustrate how spiritual truths are displayed every day in the physical world by observing and learning how plants grow and perpetuate life on this planet. This is an incredible area of science, seemingly finding new discoveries every day. But without recognition of a creator and a savior, and a life hereafter, the truth of science becomes useless—an evolution of always needing more, and never quite getting there. When will we have all the answers to plant production, food distribution, and a sustainable future?

Or, on the other hand, like me, do you fully believe that God created the heavens and the earth, as the Bible says?

"All Scripture is given by inspiration of God, and is profitable for doctrine, for reproof, for correction, for instruction in righteousness, that the man of God may be complete, thoroughly equipped for every good work." (2 Timothy 3:16)

If so, then science will never be able to fully explain exactly how the creation event took place. Does that make science a falsehood? When do we trust science and when do we trust faith? Is it possible to live and accept that both are true? This creates a paradox for the scientist. However, for someone that trusts that the Bible is the true word of God, inspired by the Holy Spirit, given for me, it is not difficult to embrace both to be true.

It is my belief that the Bible is true. The Bible then can speak in both the scientific and the spiritual sense at the same time. Science can only explain things in the physical realm. But when you have belief in a spiritual realm that is just as true and real as the physical realm (if not much more so), then science and faith can be fully complimentary. It is my prayer that as you read this discussion, you too can see how faith and science can point to the truth, not only to help us mange our farms and ranches, but also result in a strengthening of our faith in God and his Son Jesus Christ, and His plan for our salvation.

What does any of this have to do with farming? Everything. There is no one better qualified, or maybe I should say required, to make decisions by both science and faith. This is really what it comes down to in modern farming. We have incredible advancements in science. With all of the advancements in knowledge about seed genetics and traits, chemicals and fertilizers, shouldn't farming be simple? Just follow the flow chart that the smart people made, that have it all figured out. Give the seed everything it needs and harvest a big yield, right? Just follow the science!

It might work perfectly in lab conditions, but what happens when the process is subjected to weather extremes and new pests and resistant weeds? What about unpredictable markets and political upheaval? How about trade policy and risk management, climate change, and water quality issues? What about food safety and security?

It is not simple at all. Or is it? What if we looked to the Bible to help teach us how to farm? Are there answers about how we should approach farming in the Bible?

[3] **And God said, "Let there be light," and there was light.** [4] **God saw that the light was good, and he separated the light from the darkness.** [5] **God called the light "day," and the darkness he called "night." And there was evening, and there was morning—the first day.**

The very first thing God created was light. Life cannot exist without light. Notice that God had not yet created the sun and the earth. Yet there was light? Now there is a mind-bender! What was the source? Science will have trouble with that one.

Jesus describes himself in John 8:

[12] **When Jesus spoke again to the people, he said,** *"I am the light of the world. Whoever follows me will never walk in darkness, but will have the light of life."*

The connotations and descriptions about light and life are throughout the Bible. This is fully in line with both science and farming. Without light, we cannot grow anything. Light is the source of all energy on the planet. Light makes everything work. Not only does light keep our planet habitable, it provides all of our food through photosynthesis. You remember photosynthesis from high school or college biology:

$$6CO_2 + 6H_2O \xrightarrow{\text{Light}} C_6H_{12}O_6 + 6O_2$$

Carbon dioxide + Water → Sugar + Oxygen

Notice light is the energy to drive this reaction. Also, there is a complimentary reaction that takes place during hours of no light.

$$C_6H_{12}O_6 + 6O_2 \rightarrow 6CO_2 + 6H_2O + 32 \text{ ATP } (\textit{energy})$$

This is how plants remain cool and put their newly obtained energy (glucose) to work to not only provide for its growth, but also feed the microbial community that lives there. Much more on that later. But the point is, light drives the whole process. The speed and efficiency of photosynthesis is strongly influenced by light, temperature, and humidity. Can we control those things—the weather? Not unless we are farming in a greenhouse. There is not much we can do but accept what the weather gives us.

In agriculture, light is free. Water, in the form of rainfall, is free. And CO2, the source of carbon and oxygen to make these life-giving substances, is free. Nitrogen—also 78 percent of the air that plants take in during photosynthesis—is also free, though not yet fully usable by the plant. So think about it. Everything that plants need to grow and support life on this planet—is free!

We can learn a lot from this concept in the spiritual sense. Jesus Christ died on the cross and was resurrected on the third day in this physical world to forgive our sin. Is this anything you need to pay for? Can you change anything about the fact that this occurred on your behalf? No. It is free. Free to those that believe and are baptized into Jesus's name. Just as sunlight, rainfall, and humidity drive life processes in plants, without any help from us, so too did Jesus's blood shed on the cross for your redemption and salvation into eternal life—occurred without our help, for free.

No matter how hard we try to do all the right things, ultimately, it is out of our hands and fully dependent upon God. If only we can farm with that concept being the heart of how we approach it. We should get up every morning, thank and praise, serve and obey Him. Thank Him for all of His free gifts to us. This means staying in the Word, asking for guidance and thanking God for all he has done, and live your life—including how you farm to the glory of God. It is a sure way to lighten the load. As Jesus said in Matthew 1:

29 Take my yoke upon you and learn from me, for I am gentle and humble in heart, and you will find rest for your souls.

2

Water

⁶ And God said, "Let there be a vault between the waters to separate water from water." ⁷ So God made the vault and separated the water under the vault from the water above it. And it was so. ⁸ God called the vault "sky." And there was evening, and there was morning—the second day

God separated the water. It seems maybe water was present, but not under any sort of organization. This creation verse seems to indicate the creation of our atmosphere, in the form of water vapor, separated from larger expanse of liquid ocean. This created the conditions for the beginning of life. And when you think about it, all that was there was the water, light, and the Word.

The same has always been true since the beginning. The same is true today. This is a timeless gift from God. Without water and light there is no life. Farmers know this well. Likewise, without the Word, there is no life. Yes, we may see people alive in the world, but without water and the word—baptism—true life, life eternal with Christ is missing. You can easily see how this type of life—life without Christ—is similar to living in a drought.

When we see severe drought conditions on earth, it should remind us of what is important, and who is really in charge. We receive water as a gift of grace from God. God is in control of it. But water falls on the evil and the good as it states in Ecclesiastes. Ours is not to question why—we are to instead be thankful and respectful of the water we receive. It is God's gift. We should treasure it and make the most of the water we receive. In John we read Jesus's response to the woman at the well. [10]**Jesus answered, *"If you knew the generosity of God and who I am, you would be asking me for a drink, and I would give you fresh, living water."***

Water without the Word is just water. Water with the Word has the power of restoration, through baptism. We should treat water as a blessing of faith. Not everyone receives the same, but we should be thankful and make the most of the water and the faith that we are blessed to receive.

3

Land

⁹ **And God said, "Let the water under the sky be gathered to one place, and let dry ground appear." And it was so. ¹⁰ God called the dry ground "land," and the gathered waters he called "seas." And God saw that it was good**

God created the continents and separated them out from the oceans. God created land. A firmament if you will. Bedrock. Stability. Someplace to start a foundation and to build. The land was a place to build something, as well as a place to grow something. Civilization had to have a bedrock foundation on which to build and grow. Without a firm, solid, permanent bedrock foundation, the rest of the process of creation could not stand.

The same can be said about our life in Christ. It needs a solid foundation built on everlasting truth. It cannot be changeable or molded into what we want it to be. It needs to be based on something solid and unmovable and it must last forever. Without a solid truth to base our faith, our whole belief paradigm will be challenged and will not last. In the physical world, there are also some scientific truths. However, as scientists obtain a deeper understanding of physics, biology, and chemistry, new theories of how things work are discovered every day. Scientific paradigms are challenged and rewritten every day. Today, this is happening at a pace so fast that even very smart, knowledgeable people do not know what to believe anymore.

This is especially true in agriculture. Many of the things we thought we knew for sure are being questioned and challenged. In the past we have relied on university research and field trials—and that is a great place to look for information. However, there are new paradigms and questions being asked every day about things like carbon and nitrogen cycling and how plants benefit from the process. A new paradigm is being written that relies less and less on crop inputs, and more and more on the processes that can be obtained from a healthy biological community. This is the basis of the soil health movement—or regenerative agriculture if you will.

What did Jesus say to Peter?

18 And I tell you that you are Peter, and on this rock I will build my church, and the gates of Hades will not overcome it.

So, what is solid? What is something to go back to that is bedrock—where is the truth? If your faith is not based on the solid foundation of Christ, how can anything else make any sense? If everything we know for sure in the scientific world is constantly changing, where are we to go to find truth? The one place it can be found—the Bible—God's word. As Christ told Peter, nothing can ever defeat the true church built on the foundation of Christ. We live in a physical world where everything we thought for sure was truth is being questioned. Stand firm on the foundation built on the bedrock of Christ.

Someone else asked this question at a pivotal point in history, and it has been recorded for all time in John 18:

[38] **"What is truth?" retorted Pilate.**

Jesus was crucified under the authority of Pontius Pilate. Jesus had just told him who He was and testified to the truth. Pilot asked Jesus the same question many are asking today. The truth was standing right in front of him.

4

Plants

[11] **Then God said, "Let the land produce vegetation: seed-bearing plants and trees on the land that bear fruit with seed in it, according to their various kinds." And it was so.**

Now we are really getting to it. Plants and trees, fruits and seeds. Farmers and ranchers obtain their livelihood by managing plants and growing things. Even before creating Man, these things were created. Think about the Moon or Mars. As far as we know, there is no plant life in either place. Maybe someday the scientists will find plant life in a place that is beyond our current ability to look, but as for now, we have found no plant life anywhere else in the universe.

Doesn't this seem rather unlikely, that everything on earth simply evolved into the 391,000 different species of plants? Where did the seed come from? Evolution demands that stronger species survive and reproduce. But where did the first seed come from? Are all plants descendant from one plant? Where did the seed come from for the first plant? Hmmm.

Rather we should rejoice in the diversity of plant life, celebrating the complexity of it all. We should relish in amazement the process of germination and cell propagation and flowering. What a perfect way to feed the planet and cycle its nutrients. A bit later we will learn that plants are an absolute necessity for maintaining a healthy and diverse soil microbiome—which also plays a role in our own health, through the foods we eat.

In this creation verse is the first mention of trees. Trees have a very special significance in the physical realm on earth and are used as symbols of spiritual truths throughout the Bible. In Genesis, there were two specific trees mentioned by God in Eden, and God instructs Adam and Eve about them. In the garden was the tree of life and the tree of the knowledge of good and evil. Compare this with the wooden cross of Christ—made from a tree. Even here, God is pointing us to Christ as our redeemer.

Trees provide a pretty good picture of how to endure and thrive in almost any situation. The benefits from trees can be far more than just food. They also provide shade, shelter, and wildlife habitat—all of which are protective benefits from tough conditions. Trees provide fruit and nuts, essential nutritious staples for the human diet. They also provide the raw material for construction. Our forest resources are given for us to benefit in so many ways. Think of when you were a kid—can you remember climbing a particular tree? I would bet almost everyone has such a pleasant memory. Trees deserve significance and respect. We will talk more about trees in a later chapter.

Jesus used the example of growing plants from seed often. Many of his parables involved seeds, plants, and vineyards. He referenced often the work of farmers and herdsmen. There is so much to learn from these parables in that they illustrate physical truths, but more importantly spiritual truths. They are timeless and true. They are especially important for people that make their living from the land, that count on God's blessings for everything they do. We should particularly pay special attention whenever Jesus says, "For those who have ears." The depth of knowledge that can be obtained from these scriptures is really a guidebook as to how to live a blessed Christian life. We will explore more about these truths as we delve deeper into what God's Word has to say especially to "those who have ears."

5

Astronomy

[14] And God said, "Let there be lights in the vault of the sky to separate the day from the night, and let them serve as signs to mark sacred times, and days and years, [15] and let them be lights in the vault of the sky to give light on the earth." And it was so. [16] God made two great lights—the greater light to govern the day and the lesser light to govern the night. He also made the stars.

So up to this point, day four, there was light but no sun. It seems the light was being provided by the Son, as we've already discussed. But here we have the Sun and the Moon and the stars, all created to give physical light to our solar system. The Sun shines upon the earth and all the plants and allows the biological and chemical process of photosynthesis to occur. This is the physical form of light that we usually think about—separating day from night. What do you suppose the chances are of our planet Earth being just the right distance, with just the right tilt, with just the right gravity, to orbit the Sun, to create our seasons? Or what are the odds of the Moon—which I have never heard a very good explanation of where it came from—is orbiting our Earth with such precise regularity that it rules the tides and is visible in cycles in such a predictable manner. So predictable, that the early Hebrews were instructed to use the Moon to know exactly when the sacred days were to be held. The Moon was placed in our orbit to be a calendar. Also, the distance from the Earth seems to be just perfect, so that during a solar eclipse, our perspective from Earth makes the two circular objects appear the same in diameter, giving a picture of perfection. This is all just a nice celestial coincidence according to evolutionary theories.

The vastness of the universe is beyond the capability of my mind to comprehend. In fact, one of my earliest memories as a child had to do with contemplation of this vastness. I remember a recurring dream in which there was this white line out in the blackness of space. The line would double in length. Then it would double again, and again, and again. My mind was waiting for it to get to the end, where it could never double anymore, but always there was more blackness to double into. Then, suddenly, for no reason, the line would begin to cut in half. And cut in half again, and again, and again. My mind again was hoping to achieve the point of smallness that it could never be cut in half. But always there was piece of the line, left to be cut in half.

I would wake up in a somewhat panicked state of mind and try to explain to my parents what was going on in this nightmare.

I think about this now, and it still makes me uncomfortable. What is infinity? What is eternity? Are these things something to fear? To the human mind—at least to this one—these questions are unanswerable to us in this physical world, much of which can be explained by science. However, I have found comfort with the realization that in this world those questions will never be answered. Only in the spiritual world—where time and space do not exist as we know them—will those concepts begin to be understood. It is like looking into the mind of God. Most of us do not have the mental capacity. Usually, for questions that are unanswerable like these, our mind conveniently and quickly moves on to more tangible concepts. Suffice it to say as St. Paul said in Romans 11:

[33] **Oh, the depth of the riches both of the wisdom and knowledge of God! How unsearchable *are* His judgments and unsearchable are His ways!**

6

Birds and Fish

20 And God said, "Let the water teem with living creatures, and let birds fly above the earth across the vault of the sky." 21 So God created the great creatures of the sea and every living thing with which the water teems and that moves about in it, according to their kinds, and every winged bird according to its kind.

This is day five of creation. God creates everything that lives in the water, and the birds. I have not looked it up, but the number of species of fish and birds is a very big number. The water is teeming with life. The birds are of all shapes and sizes, colors, and sounds. The diversity of species—each according to its kind—is quite a blessing for planet earth. Can you imagine a sky with no birds? How about an ocean with no fish? These things should be cherished and treasured. There is something very grand about this vast diversity.

It is clear the fish and the birds were here before us. What does that say about them? Are they important? God created these species for our pleasure and enjoyment, as well as to serve as future source for food and our survival. In order to continue to have the benefits that all these creatures provide for humankind, the places where they live and the quality of their habitat need to be respected and cared for. This is just basic stewardship. We need to be careful not to pollute our environment or over-harvest birds or fish. Doing so results in a world that is not as pleasurable to live in. Loss of diversity means loss of joy. Future generations will not be able to enjoy these creations, if we fail to ensure they are cared for and respected. These species require our attention and consideration.

When species of birds or fish become extinct, it means we have failed to respect creation. Whenever creation is not respected, there are likely to be negative consequences. Not respecting creation is the same as disrespecting the creator. How we manage creation says a lot about how we treat each other. If we fail to respect each other, we are really disrespecting our creator. Diversity is the spice of life. It does not mean we will always agree, but it does require respect for each other's perspective. Sometimes, a situation may be presented to witness to Christ. As written in Romans 10:

[14] How, then, can they call on the one they have not believed in? And how can they believe in the one of whom they have not heard? And how can they hear without someone preaching to them? [15] And how can anyone preach unless they are sent? As it is written: "How beautiful are the feet of those who bring good news!"[g]

Here is an opportunity for a Christian to provide witness to a non-believer with regards to taking care of our environment and the diversity it provides. It also speaks to how we should treat each other—also respecting the diversity among us. After all, are we not all God's creation? Didn't Christ die for all people's sins? Wasn't this gift given to people of all races, opinions, and beliefs? The reconciliation of Christ really leaves little excuse for disrespect of diversity. Rather, it is the job of the Christian to tell this good news to others and live a life worthy of the name. These are people with beautiful feet, walking a straight path, and enlarging Christ's kingdom for the bountiful harvest that lies ahead.

7

Animals

[24] And God said, "Let the land produce living creatures according to their kinds: the livestock, the creatures that move along the ground, and the wild animals, each according to its kind." And it was so. [25] God made the wild animals according to their kinds, the livestock according to their kinds, and all the creatures that move along the ground according to their kinds. And God saw that it was good.

Now we are on day six of creation. This is a big day. This is the day that God brings into existence all the land animals, both wild and domestic. Of course, evolutionary theory would suggest that domesticated animals were all tamed through millions of years of man and beast evolving toward some sort of natural progression. It really does not make logical sense when you think about it. Take a cow for example. What wild animal would devolve into a domesticated state to become a cow? Would a brontosaurus—simply decide to not be so mean, and change its attitude, and decide to settle down, eat plants, and give milk for the caveman? Would a wildebeest give up its migration instinct to live in an overgrazed pasture and be herded around by man instead? How does all of that happen exactly?

The creation narrative seems more plausible to me, that wild and domesticated animals were created that way and placed on this earth before man, so that they could provide the necessities of life for humankind. Not that they are simply to be dominated and put into submission and service, but instead to be wisely managed and provided for and given full respect through proper animal husbandry. These animals are some of God's greatest gifts for us. They help us see the beauty of creation and reproduction, life and death. Purpose, for our lives, is illustrated very plainly through a domesticated animal's presence in our lives. Take for example a favorite pet like a hunting dog. They live and have been bred toward a very specific purpose—to locate and retrieve game to assist humans. Those instincts are fine-tuned to make both dog and man successful. It creates a very special bond—as does any special pet—between man and beast.

But a good hunting dog usually does not live as long as its owner. It has one purpose, and that is to please its master. In return, the master feeds and cares for it. These acts are part of a vibrant and fulfilling life. When that life is over, true sorrow is experienced. These are special moments and should trigger a tearful response of respect and admiration for God's gifts to us. It also teaches us much about how to treat each other, with respect for His creation of each of us. This is love for one another. Life itself is sacred. It should be treasured, cared for, and appreciated through love. If life is diminished to something that simply evolved—survival of the fittest—then true pleasures in life like having pets and raising livestock are missing. Survival of the fittest does not demand respect or appreciation for animals. They are not gifts at all…just meat. Lifeless, loveless McNuggets. I am not suggesting vegetarianism, but rather respect for the animals that we were given, both domestic and wild…each of its own kind.

8

Souls

At some point during day six, God decided to create man…in his own image.

This is God's crowning moment of all his wonderful work, a man, made to care for and enjoy everything that was created. What good would creation have been if there were not a man to enjoy it? Why would God create all this wonderful universe, unless he could share it with someone? Man was not equal to God but rather created and placed on the earth, in order to worship and love him in return. This is to be displayed in how we treat his creation, and how we are to treat each other—with love. As such, God gave man a special gift—that was in his own image—a soul. Each of us has a soul—a very real spiritual connection to God, our creator. How we care for that gift—our soul—determines the extent of the growth and maturity of the faith we have been given from God. Keeping the connection strong, vibrant, and lively is fully to our own benefit. On the contrary, neglect for our soul will result in a lessening of that spiritual connection. The soul is something that is very real and must be tended with deliberate care. There is a remarkable—unbelievable really—comparison between care for the soul…and care for the soil. Both of God's creation, both with invisible but very real characteristics, and both very alive. How we manage the soil can be equated with how we manage our soul. God has given us the principles. It is up to us whether we want to listen. Do you have ears?

9

Rest

On the seventh day, God rested. This is a day set aside for us, to take pause, regroup, listen to the Lord, and to thank and praise him for all that He has done, and worship Him. It is important to do, and not something to take lightly as God has commanded us to Remember the Sabbath and to keep it Holy. It is always wise to listen to God's instructions. We ought to find time to do this every day, but taking one day a week off from your normal work schedule is the example given to us by God. Failure to do so will catch up to you in ways we may not always recognize. Health, both physical and spiritual, will suffer, as well as relationships with others, potentially leading toward additional stress. Financial gains from a workaholic lifestyle will be fleeting. It's not worth it. You may be gaining in one aspect of your physical life, but you are missing out on some aspects of a healthy spiritual life, by neglecting the word and sacraments, offered for free, at least once a week on a day of rest. Hearing the word is how we strengthen our faith, and to thank God for sending His son as a sacrifice for our sin. We were created to love Him, and finding time in our busy lives to stop and reprioritize our thinking about truly important things are what give us strength and renewal to begin another week, knowing we have heard the words of forgiveness—that will provide peace beyond our understanding. Why would we not want to receive that?

10

The Soul and the Soil

When God created man, he did so in a different manner than simply saying, "Let there be." Instead, the Bible goes into a bit more specific detail as to several important actions that God took in the act of creating man. Read carefully the words in Genesis chapter 2:

⁷ Then the Lord God formed a man[c] from the dust of the ground and breathed into his nostrils the breath of life, and the man became a living being.

This passage is the key to understanding who we are as humans, separate from animals yet formed from the dust of the ground. Envision God reaching down to the ground, cupping a handful of the earth, bringing it up to his mouth and breathing life into it, creating Man. This action turned the dust…into man. It turned the dust…into soil, and the soil into a soul. Soil to soul. This was in Eden, before sin, and it was perfect. What was the difference between dust and soil? Remember, God says in Genesis 3:19:

After the fall of man, God said,

By the sweat of your face You shall eat bread, Until you return to the ground, Because from it you were taken; For you are dust, And to dust you shall return."

There is the proof of who we are, how we were made, and where we will end up. We are all going to die. The difference of what happens next is determined by the health of our soul.

It is truly remarkable the comparisons that can be made between soil health management and soul health management. The equivalencies are clearly made in Genesis. We are made from soil. Throughout the Bible, the theme of soil and soul is displayed over and over. Jesus's parables in the New Testament are often related to agronomic principles with the soil being the common theme. The process of getting a harvest requires specific steps. Planning a crop involves seed selection, field location, planting operations, paying attention to threats, nutrition, and finally harvest, and storage. There are parables given in Jesus's own words that relate to each of these processes, that also relate to our faith, and ultimately our soul. Mostly the success of our efforts relates to how well we manage the free gifts we are given from heaven.

Soul (Soil) Health

We are hearing a tremendous amount of talk and press about soil health. What is it? How do we define it? Can it be measured? Isn't the soil just something we grow a crop in and then prepare for another crop the next year? Why should we worry about soil health?

Jesus made an astounding statement about soil health when he gave us this parable in Luke 8, from the parable of the sower:

"A farmer went out to sow his seed. As he was scattering the seed, some fell along the path; it was trampled on, and the birds ate it up. [6] Some fell on rocky ground, and when it came up, the plants withered because they had no moisture. [7] Other seed fell among thorns, which grew up with it and choked the plants. [8] Still other seed fell on good soil. It came up and yielded a crop, a hundred times more than was sown."

When he said this, he called out, "Whoever has ears to hear, let them hear."

[9] His disciples asked him what this parable meant. [10] He said, "The knowledge of the secrets of the kingdom of God has been given to you, but to others I speak in parables, so that,

"'though seeing, they may not see; though hearing, they may not understand.'[a]

[11] "This is the meaning of the parable: The seed is the word of God. [12] Those along the path are the ones who hear, and then the devil comes and takes away the word from their hearts, so that they may not believe and be saved. [13] Those on the rocky ground are the ones who receive the word with joy when they hear it, but they have no root. They believe for a while, but in the time of testing they fall away. [14] The seed that fell among thorns stands for those who hear, but as they go on their way they are choked by life's worries, riches and pleasures, and they do not mature. [15] But the seed on good soil stands for those with a noble and good heart, who hear the word, retain it, and by persevering produce a crop."

What does this have to do with healthy soil? Soil is the very word that Jesus uses to illustrate the comparison———meaning both are correct. How we manage for a healthy soil is illustrated exactly as the same way we should manage our lives for a healthy soul.

What an awesome description of what can happen in the physical world as characterized by seed, and what it takes to grow a crop to successful harvest. Then Christ describes the meaning of the parable in a clear way to His disciples. But did you catch it? "Whoever has ears, let them hear."

Doesn't everyone have ears? What are ears used for?

Ears were given to Man at creation as the way for Man to hear. What does it mean to hear? This is where it relates so well to our soul—to hear is to receive. Ears do one thing—receive. Most everyone is capable of hearing, but what are you to do with the information? This is the key…a perfect description of how to keep your soul healthy, leading to a noble and good heart, by retaining the Word, persevering, and producing a harvest.

In the same way, soil does one thing—it receives. The soil is like our ears. All soil is not the same, yet all soil is capable of producing a good yield if it is managed and cared for in manner that receives, rather than simply viewed as being a substrate for crops to grow in. Healthy soil has life. Healthy soil needs to receive in order to produce. It needs seed, to grow a plant. Plants provide the soil with the necessary means to collect the carbon, oxygen, and nitrogen from the atmosphere, combined with water and turn it into a harvest. A healthy soil can only do this with an incredibly complex diverse community of microbes that live in the soil if it is managed properly. This is all driven by light. The efficiency of the system is determined by how well we as caretakers manage these free gifts. How much free plant nutrition do you want? The more free nutrients the plant receives, the more it can produce a big harvest.

On the other hand, we tend to think as farmers we need to provide these things. Most of this comes from the idea of the "law of the minimum." Soil fertility experts agree that yield is limited by the nutrient that is in least supply. As a result, we soil test and apply amendments and strive to build nutrient levels to luxury levels, thinking that is how we will maximize yield. Is that process utilizing the free gifts to their fullest potential? Yes, the soil is receiving, but there is a cost. It is not free.

Why is the soil in need of nutrients? It depends. It could be that the soil has effectively been mined over many years of misguided management. It could be that the soil is inherently poor nutritionally, due its geographic morphology or local orientation—in other words it was created that way.

It could be that the soil and the environmental conditions are not ideally suited to grow one or two crops commodity crops, in the manner that we would like to grow them. The soil might be better suited for grazing or forestry purposes. It could be that the soil is prone to saturation or flooding. It is one of mankind's favorite pastimes, to see if we can improve God's creation to make the soil do something we want it to do, rather than use it the way God intended it to be used. Whenever we conduct a major disturbance in the soil, attempting to improve it, there will be consequences.

But Christ describes a healthy soil as compared to a healthy soul. In order to produce a hundredfold, it must be managed in a very specific manner. The soil must be in a condition to receive the seed. His explanation of the parable of the sower gives us a very precise prescription for a successful outcome. The seed, once it has been sown, can be susceptible to various outcomes. Sometimes it is eaten or stolen and never gets a chance to sprout. It might fall into a place with little or no soil to take root and grow. This seed it very susceptible to stresses like drought or heat and never comes into maturity. Next, He describes seed that is outcompeted by undesirable plants like weeds or thorns. It never grows to provide the full harvest potential, either. Finally, the seed which lies in good soil, comes to full maturity and produces a hundredfold. How should we manage the seed that we receive to plant? It is just a haphazard effort of simply tossing the seed in the air and hoping it falls on good soil? We do not usually farm that way (although nature tends to reseed itself using that method).

To get a great harvest, we should use the methods Christ describes. We should limit the potential for the soil to be disturbed, we should protect the seed from threats, we should reduce competition from undesirable plants, and we should trust that God is in charge, and we are at his mercy. The harvest is left up to him, but we must follow and trust His methods. It requires a good and faithful heart that can withstand outside influences and be steadfast in the truth to be able to persevere. The parable is about how we manage our heart and soul, so that we can provide a harvest for Him, not for ourselves. If we do that, he promises to provide everything we need—no matter the circumstances. All we really need is Christ's grace. Are we willing to receive it and use it to God's glory for His harvest? Do you have ears?

The next chapters of this book will explore those comparisons, and hopefully bring into reality how the job of a Christian farmer is to receive God's grace, through light, to grow and care for his kingdom—and help to bring in His harvest. How is this done? Well, if we look in God's instruction book—the Bible—to us…a "Christian soul owner's manual' if you will, it is full of instruction as well as some basic principles to follow. In John Stika's book *A Soil Owner's Manual*, four (or five) basic principles for how to manage soil for better function are outlined. The premise is that how we have managed our soils in the past is not leading us toward a sustainable future of production from our soils. In fact, just the opposite. Our adoption and dependance upon chemistry and science based purely on outcomes has taken us down a path of dependance on crop inputs that may produce yield, but fail to allow the living, breathing biological community that lives in the soil to thrive. It has largely been ignored, neglected, and destroyed. This was not necessarily intentional, but because this biologically community cannot easily be seen, it is easy to neglect.

What happens to our faith if it is neglected? It, too, is not always obviously seen. Can anyone look at you and instantly recognize that you are a person of strong faith? How is one to tell? Are there any visual signs or indicators? Are your actions representative of a thankful life in Christ, living under His grace toward His glory? Can someone put a spade into your life, exposing your structure to see if you are functioning at a healthy, high level?

That is the best way that we can test our soil for function. After several years of implementation and adoption of the soil health principles, turning over a spadeful of soil will show restoration of function as well as indications of regeneration. Those soil health principles have been developed to help guide us toward restoration and regeneration of soil function, through recognition and management of the living, breathing biological community that was in the soil at creation, and is still there today. Plants are necessary to maintain healthy soil. The biological community lives and thrives in healthy soil. Soil is the common denominator.

We can grow most plants in hydroponic systems, without soil. We can also remove biology from soil and provide everything a plant needs artificially. It takes a lot of water and energy to do that. This method of production neglects the free biology. It must be supplemented. On the other hand, a healthy soil with a full complement of biological diversity and function can provide everything a plant needs as a result of the relationships that the microbial community can make between soil and plants. Those relationships and the benefits they bring to plant production can be obtained through the following soil health principles:

Reduce Disturbance

Protect the Soil Surface

Provide Diversity

Keep Living Roots as much as possible

Incorporate Animal Benefits

If these are in fact "principles," wouldn't the Bible have something to say about them? The next chapters will explore each one of these principles and discover that the Bible does have something to say about them. Can principled management of our soil also display principled management of our soul? Can the actions we take to manage our soil fall in line with how we manage our soul? God gave us the Ten Commandments in Exodus through Moses. The primary purpose of the Ten Commandments was to give the basic rules for living a life with the right priorities in your heart. They were the set of laws, true for all time, under which all of mankind was to live. Violation of these laws constitute sin. So not only were the Ten Commandments a set of laws, but they were also a mirror. They show us our sin, and then need for repentance. When the laws are broken, there are consequences. No man can keep them perfectly. That shows us our need for a savior. The commandments show us our sin and bring us back to Jesus for repentance and forgiveness. This is the Christian life.

While the soil health principles certainly are not commandments, they do function in a very similar way. Whenever the soil is not functioning up to its full capacity, something has happened that has violated one or several of the soil health principles. While there are only five of them, no matter what problem the soil may be experiencing, it can be attributed to a failure to comply with the underlying principles. While no farmer can keep them perfectly, a regenerative farmer tries to do the best he can. In doing so, there will be mistakes and failures, but the recognition as to why these failures occur also lead to more appreciation and understanding of the principles. In a way, we come to a repentant heart of realization, that something we did or have done is in violation of some underlying facts about how the soil works. We try shortcuts, chemicals, quick-fixes, and amendments, but all that is really needed is a better understanding of the principles, and the commitment to try to keep them. Restoration of the soil function will provide a rich harvest. This is what we should be striving to do as farmers. It is healthy for the soil, and for the soul. Remember, "From dust we were created, and to dust we shall return." What we do during that period while we live this life—that we are given—will determine what happens next.

11

Disturbance

⁵ And every plant of the field before it was in the earth, and every herb of the field before it grew: for the Lord God had not caused it to rain upon the earth, and there was not a man to till the ground.

This Bible verse from chapter two in Genesis presents the picture of perfection. In Eden, the perfect creation—which is a picture of heaven—describes the natural world and how it functioned in perfection. It seems that there was ample water to grow everything, without the need for rainfall. Man had not yet been created, and there was no need to grow anything for food to feed the animals or a need to care for them in any way. There was no hunger, want, or death. It was a time of perfect creation before sin had entered the world. Yet God was not done. He wanted to create a special being to love and worship him, so that He could care for and love him in return.

So, as we described earlier, he took a handful of dirt, blew his life-giving breath into it, and created a soul (soil). And thankfully, so that Man would not be alone, he created a woman out of man. He gave them all the means to procreate, with instructions to multiply. All was perfect. No need to work, no need to plant, no need to harvest, no need to worry. All they had to do was bask in the amazing garden of creation and enjoy it. It was like a never-ending journey of exploring and discovering God's grace.

Man's only job was to keep an eye on things. He was placed in the garden and told to dress it and keep it. "Just don't eat of that one particular tree," were his direct instructions from God. We know what happened next. Sin entered the world, and everything changed. This was the first and most destructive disturbance. There were unavoidable consequences. It is just the nature of God's creation. There cannot be sin without consequences, and it is punishable by death. There cannot be sin in a perfect world. As long as there is sin in the world, it will be imperfect.

So man was removed from the garden of perfection, and placed into the world with a new set of responsibilities.

Cursed is the ground because of you; With [h]hard labor you shall eat *from* it All the days of your life. 18 Both thorns and thistles it shall grow for you; Yet you shall eat the [i]plants of the field; 19 By the sweat of your face You shall eat bread, Until you return to the ground, Because from it you were taken; For you are dust, And to dust you shall return."

Notice how things have changed. Now, man was given work to do to sustain himself and his animals. Now, man had to depend on God to send rainfall, to water the earth. In an imperfect world, we need to depend on God more than ever to sustain our livelihood. He still wants our love and worship and promises to love us in return, but we will still need to deal with sin and figure out how to live in this corrupted world, with all its thorns and thistles.

Man failed to follow God's instructions—"to dress and to keep" his garden. Adam and Eve had allowed Satan to deceive them. This was the first and most disruptive event. It was a great disturbance to God's creation and the fabric of our relationship with God.

Consider a similar analogy of a great disturbance in the soil. There are many ways to disturb the soil. Deep tillage, chemical applications, pesticides and fungicides. Every one of these can be considered a great disturbance to the vast biological community that lives in the soil. A healthy soil is a huge community—with billions of organisms that are all present to serve a specific purpose. Great disturbances cause major disruptions to that community, greatly affecting the ability of that community to conduct its work. Imagine if a large tornado were to go through your hometown. Quite often, many people rally behind the community to begin clean-up efforts and to rebuild. What if that tornado hits every year? At some point, people would give up and move on. This is what is happening to the biological community in the soil with every major disturbance.

That is why one of the principles of soil health is to "Limit Disturbance." We cannot continue to disturb the soil continually and expect it to not have very significant consequences. Disturbances set the biological community back to stage one, which is to eat, reproduce, and build. Soil bacteria are the first microbes to respond and begin that process. Bacteria need to eat, reproduce, and start the processes of building. They do this by consuming a diet of nutrients that suit their ideal condition with a balance of nitrogen and carbon. This process is called immobilization. Nutrients are taken up into microbes and are not available for plants until the microbes die or are eaten and give them up. Other microbes such as protozoa eat bacteria and process many of those nutrients in a similar manner, dying or being eaten by larger critters such as nematodes and earthworms. This is a very simplified discussion, but this is the mineralization process by which humus is made. Humus is the stable form of carbon that is necessary to form stable organic matter in our soils.

When soils are continually disturbed, these fully biological, natural processes are disrupted, and set back to stage one—ideal conditions for a huge flush of bacteria eating the newly available carbon and nitrogen. In the case of tillage, a vast release of CO_2 is given up to the atmosphere, as the bacterial flush begins eating and reproducing, eating everything that is available, including prior crop residues. This massive bacterial population must breathe. They exhale CO2. With conventional tillage agriculture, it is extremely difficult to build organic matter, because the microbes never get a chance to build it. They are constantly being set back to the first stage. Also, now you can see why over a couple of generations of tillage, soil organic matter declines and the percentage of CO2 concentration in the atmosphere increases. This is the basis for promotion of regenerative agriculture. How can we slow this conversion? Can we not only slow it, but reverse it?

Now think about disturbance in your life. Sin and temptation are always lurking. What happens if we become complacent to it, and in fact maybe become comfortable with it. Quite often, we find ways to justify our actions in our minds, and after a while or a few years we may become so comfortable and ignorant to sin that it can become part of our being. Oh, how we love the smell and the appearance of freshly turned, black soil! It can be addictive.

When we lose a sense of guilt or shame about our sin, we are in danger of losing the promises that God gave us at creation. We are instructed to guard and keep our relationship with Him and limit the disturbances. Failure to do so keeps us at square one. We will never get to experience the full potential of the joy of living in a mature relationship with Him. The Christian life is meant to be joyful and fruitful. The pathway to that joy begins with recognizing disturbances, repenting, receiving forgiveness, and then resetting the process toward trying to do better.

When it comes to management of our soils, tillage is a major disturbance. I recently wrote a one-page document, the purpose of which is to illustrate what happens to the soil as result of tillage. It is intended to make you think twice before choosing tillage as a management option.

What would you do to the soil,
If you want to increase runoff? Till.

If you want to increase compaction? Till.

If you want to see more gully erosion? Till.

If you want to expose your soil to the effects of pounding rain? Till.

If you want to reduce the biological community? Till.

If you want to expose your soil to heat and cold extremes? Till.

If you want to starve your soil microbes? Till.

If you want to pond water? Till.

If you want to increase evaporation to draw up salts to the soil surface? Till.

If you want to speed up loss of organic matter? Till.

If you want to make sure you have a fresh weed flush? Till.

If you want to compact the surface of your soil to promote crusting? Till.

If you want make sure you have huge variability in your zone mapping system? Till.

If you want to put more CO2, NO2, and CH4 into the atmosphere, and remove C and N from the soil? Till.

If you want to make sure you are increasing your acres of prevent plant payments? Till.

If you want to have higher crop insurance premiums? Till.

If you want to make sure you are increasing your fuel and fertilizer expenses? Till.

If you want to invest in machinery expenses that will ultimately reduce your long-term yields? Till.

If you want to increase input costs and reduce income? Till.

If you don't consider much about a future generation trying to make a living off your land? Till.

On the other hand,
Reduce tillage and disturbance
Keep living roots
Increase diversity

Protect the soil surface
Utilize livestock and manure

You and the next farmer might have a chance.

I am not saying that tillage or using fertilizer and chemicals is sinful. I am saying that disturbances have consequences. We may think we are seeing positive results from our actions, but constant disturbances slow and inhibit our progress toward a fully functioning soil. Just as it is difficult to build "humus" in our "soil," disturbance slows and inhibits progress toward a fully functioning "soul" in our "human" condition. It is not by accident that soil and soul, and humus and human are spelled so similarly.

Do we as Christian farmers tend to go to church on Sunday and then back to farming on Monday? Or maybe we even skip worship it when it seems we are crunched for time to get the seed in the ground, or the fertilizer spread, or get the crop in the bin. If we cannot find time to tend, guard, or keep our relationship with God because we are too busy farming to feed the world, then maybe it is time to evaluate our situation. Has God given us too many acres to cover? Has he blessed us with too much to do, so much so that we cannot take time to rest for one day and worship and give thanks for all that we have? It is all God's in the first place, and it is all His in the end. Our job is to tend it and keep it. You are the Adam of the garden. Are you too distracted with disturbances to even recognize your sinful condition?

Take heart. Christ has given His life and has dealt with our sinful condition for us. We know this and believe it. Christ is the pathway to regeneration. We just need to accept it, and begin living in a manner that glorifies him, letting him build the organic matter of our souls, so that we may be fruitful. All we need to do is accept his light and life-giving water. Water and the Word, His blood and His bread are all we need to stay on task and limit the potential effects of disturbance. Can you make the sun shine? Can you make it rain? Can you make humus? Can you make plants grow? We can do none of these things. Our job is to keep it and tend it. It begins by recognizing who created it in the first place, and then stop thinking we can improve it or do it better than God did it. We should rather accept His grace, through His Son Jesus Christ, and then go about our assignment of tending and keeping His garden for his glory. His garden is our soul, and our relationship with Him is through His Son. Anything else is unsustainable.

So, is all disturbance sinful? Absolutely not. We still must deal with thorns and thistles. This is part of the tending and keeping. Is it sinful to use a non-selective herbicide to kill weeds? Is it sinful to apply a fungicide to prevent stress and disease at planting? How about disking to prepare the ground for seeding? If these things are considered major disturbances, how else are we to manage these agronomic problems?

The key here, when it comes to farming, is to limit how often these major disturbances occur. Using the tools that science has given us to improve our systems of management are very wise and prudent use of these gifts. However, have we taken some of these things too far and developed systems of dependency upon the tools, rather than looking at treating and anticipating the root causes? It is very tempting to see a successful outcome from applications of chemistry and then begin to think we have found all the answers.

A good example: We have glyphosate-tolerant crops and spraying systems that have been tremendously successful at reducing weed pressure and growing our cash crops, all with reduced input costs and allowing a reduction in the use of tillage. These are very good things and seem to fall in line with the principle of reducing tillage. Adoption of this system might be one of the quickest changes to be fully accepted in the history of agriculture. It has worked and has worked very well. The results have been clear, evidenced through big yields and successful outcomes. Even the skeptics must admit that this is an amazing system to grow plants and large-scale adoption of the system has become the standard for production. However, we replaced tillage (disturbance) with chemistry and genetic engineering (also disturbance).

As we now know, along came glyphosate-resistant weeds (thorns and thistles?). It is becoming very difficult to use the same system to address the same problems because we have become dependent upon that system, rather than looking deeper at the reasons for the problems. So, the question becomes, how are we going to deal with it? More chemistry? Go back to tillage? Start over?

No matter how we view it, a disturbance is going to be required. A new approach must be taken to the problem, and it will be up to us to choose that approach. Do you see how dependance upon disturbance can cause more disturbance? It is not sustainable. However, we can use disturbance to our advantage, to reset, and try a new approach—a regenerative concept.

The same is true in our spiritual lives and how we must manage our soul. Have we become complacent and comfortable with keeping our spiritual life and our work life separate? Are we prepared spiritually for disruptions and disturbances in our lives that will come? How about sudden unexpected health issues? What about COVID-19? Are we prepared spiritually to handle these types of disturbances? Have we become dependent upon things other than God, to make ourselves feel safe and comfortable? Have we insulated ourselves enough from sin, that it no longer causes us a sense of guilt? Have we written our own ethics so that we can ignore our sin?

Throughout all of history, God uses disturbances to get man's attention. Read the history of God's people, Israel. They continually were back and forth with God, and every time they wandered from His instruction, a major disturbance occurred to bring them back. God uses disturbance to bring us back to full dependance on Him. It forces us to change. If we fail to change, we will be stuck in our own problems. He uses disturbance to fine-tune and refine our souls toward worship and thankfulness for His grace. Everything in this world is His, including you. He has given us His own Son and His Holy Spirit to help us deal with the disturbances that will come to all of us. We can depend on him for obtaining true comfort and peace that only he can provide. Science can give us some tools, but we should not become fully dependent upon them. As long as there is sin in the world there will be thorns and thistles. How we deal with them is our purpose in life. Back to Jesus's parable, you are here to produce a harvest. Do you have ears?

12

Protection for the Soil

In Jesus's parable of the sower, He describes how seed (the Word of God) is sown in various conditions (our heart, or soul). The very first condition is a seed that has fallen on the path, is trampled, and is eaten by birds. It never has a chance. He then equates this with the devil coming and taking the Word away from our hearts, so that we never believe and can be saved. We never mature to be part of His harvest. How might we prevent this from happening? We must guard our hearts and minds, with the tools that God gives us. Just like a seed must be in good soil to come to harvest—it must be protected. What must we do to provide maximum protection for the seeds we plant? If we expect to get a great harvest, shouldn't we do everything we can to protect our biggest investment? Let's take a look at how we use protection—one of the soil health principles—in how we farm.

What does it mean to protect the soil? It might be easier to describe what happens when we fail to protect the soil. Unprotected soil is vulnerable to many threats most of which are outside of your control. Unprotected soil is naked. Think of how you would be vulnerable to the elements of nature if you were totally naked, outside, all the time. You would be too cold, too hot, sunburnt, frostbit, etc. Same for the soil. Unprotected, it is exposed to the same extremes. Residue on the soil surface is the best way to protect it from these extremes. "Residue is your friend"— a statement Dr. Dwayne Beck from Dakota Lakes Research Farm coined many years ago. He is one of the world's experts in teaching how to adopt no-till systems in order to keep your residue and protect the soil surface. Residue management is almost as important toward the health of your soil and the proper cycling of nutrients as anything else we can do. Removal of the residue will leave the soil unprotected.

When a soil is unprotected, it is prone to being lost. Soil and organic matter cannot be built if it is being lost. If we are losing soil, eventually you will be out of business. This has happened throughout history many times, as we see once grand and powerful civilizations begin slow decline and eventually disappear. This is well documented in Dr. David Montgomery's book *Dirt*. A civilization cannot support itself if it destroys the ability of its soil to function. When this happens, people must move to more productive soils. In today's world, this is happening at a tremendous pace as places like Brazil and Argentina have become the latest places to open to conventional agriculture, in order to feed places like China, who are unable to support their own population. It presents quite a dilemma. You can see how protection of the soil really has national security implications. A nation that protects its soils will be able to maintain their function and ability to produce. On the other hand, unprotected soils and the loss of production capabilities will destroy a nation.

When a soil is protected, its exposure to the powerful energies of wind and rain is reduced. By keeping the soil covered with the previous crops' residue or with living plants, the energy from rain or wind it absorbed by those materials, and the soil stays put. Conversely, an exposed soil can be severely impacted by these energies, usually resulting in the soil aggregation being destroyed, and allowing the particles to be set in motion. Soil can easily be blown away, or it can move with the water in runoff. These aggregates become small particles that can disperse and fill all the air channels that the soil biology has been working so hard to build and maintain. Again, the biological community will have to start all over if the soil aggregation has been destroyed. The soil becomes susceptible to all the same bad things that tillage causes.

Soil armor provides protection in other ways. Many studies have proven that a layer of residue insulates the soil from temperature extremes. It acts like a blanket in cold weather, and shade in hot weather. Stabilizing the temperature of the soil is critically important for young roots of plants to develop. Extreme daily temperature variations cause all kinds of stress to young plants, as they regulate their energy to protect from those stresses rather than use the energy for growth. Too much stress and the plant will die. It is far better to allow the protective layer of residue to help regulate those stresses.

Soil residue acts as a shade layer to prevent soils from losing moisture. A black soil on a sunny day can absorb a lot of radiant energy from the sun. This causes water to draw toward the surface through evaporation. Evaporated water is water that no longer available for plants. It is lost. The other issue with evaporation is it leaves behind whatever is dissolved in the water on the surface. This is readily seen as a white layer of salt left on the soil surface. This is one of the quickest ways to destroy the ability of the soil to function. Worsening salinity will cause a drought situation for plants and seeds, such that they may not even be able to germinate. It is not a good idea, if an area is starting to indicate salinity, to till or disk up the area. It only makes the situation worse. The presence of weeds in these areas is nature's way of trying to correct the situation. It can only be reversed by having a plant that can eventually provide residue to protect the soil surface to prevent future evaporation.

The nature of soil is to protect itself. A black tilled soil is not present in nature, unless a catastrophic event such as a wildfire, an earthquake, or slumping. After these events, plants begin to grow almost immediately.

The soil protects itself by providing the perfect opportunity for early successional plants to establish and take hold. This is the way to reset the process. First shallow-rooted plants, then residues, then microbes, then soil aggregation, then deeper-rooted plants and then full soil function and regenerative capabilities. Why would we want to get in the way, and start that process over? Weeds are nature's way of starting over. An exposed soil will grow weeds. Our instinct says to kill the weeds—we would not want them going to seed, so we till or burn. Now we have started over—leaving the soil prone to more weeds. It is better to allow the weeds to provide residue, kill them, and plant a desirable crop into the residue. This will keep the weed pressure down in the long run.

When soil aggregates are broken down by the erosive energies of rain and wind, what remains is are individual particles of sand, silt, clay, and organic matter. These materials will move and form layers on the surface of the soil and clog all the macro and micro pores. These visible layers become crusted and can prevent water infiltration and germination. When soils are crusting this is an indication of erosion due to exposure. This is how compaction begins. Again, our instinct is to disk up that compaction, but really, we would just be perpetuating the situation—leaving the soil even more exposed. The best way to prevent this is to maintain residue, and more living roots.

Residue on the surface is where the microbes live that can break down the residues and begin the process of building soil aggregates. Removal or destruction of that critical layer destroys the habitat that those microbes need. Keeping a protective layer on the soil is the key to maintaining a healthy soil. Without protection, the soil does not function very well.

What does the Bible have to say about protecting our soul? Is it important? What are the threats? What are the benefits of protection? Who should we look to for protection?

13

Protection for the Soul

The first mention of protection is in the Garden of Eden, when God instructs Man to tend the garden. This includes keeping your guard up for threats. Of course, you know the story, the Devil tempted Eve, and then Adam to eat of the one tree they were not to eat from. They let their guard down. They ate, and sin entered the world. But what was Adam and Eve's very first response?

7 Then the eyes of both of them were opened, and they realized they were naked; so they sewed fig leaves together and made coverings for themselves.

Prior to this event, they did not care that they were naked. In fact, they did not even know they were naked. They had full protection from God before they sinned.

11 And he said, "Who told you that you were naked?

They now felt very ashamed and wanted to hide themselves from God. They knew they had violated God's law. They tried to hide from their sin and cover up their nakedness. But where did the fig leaves come from in the first place? They were God's creation. Then, after God found them and confronted them with their sin, what did he do? He had to ban them from the garden because no sin can be in the garden. Adam and Eve now had to live in a sinful, imperfect world, outside of God's perfection. But God did not leave them helpless and naked.

²¹ The LORD God made garments of skin for Adam and his wife and clothed them.

God knew that the fig leaves were not good enough. He made them garments of animal skin. This required the shedding of blood, a sacrifice if you will, for Adam and Eve's protection (also pointing to Christ's blood sacrifice for us). God gave them what they now needed, provisions to live in an imperfect world. God took further action and gave them further instructions:

²³ So the LORD God banished him from the Garden of Eden to work the ground from which he had been taken.

God tasked them with having to work in order to eat. Currently, Adam and Eve's diet was still vegetarian. But they were now going to have to manage plants growing outside of the garden, in order to harvest their food. This was the beginning of agriculture. It was the very first profession given to man. Cain and Able were Adam and Eve's twin sons. Cain was a farmer, and Able was a shepherd. Having to work was an interesting result of sin, because of man's failure to protect himself from temptation. But God gave man everything he needed to protect his soul. Whether Man chooses to use those protections is up to him. Failure to protect the soul, just like failure to protect the soil, likely will have negative consequences.

So what does God specifically tell us to do to protect our soul? The first thing He did was give them the means to clothe themselves. Just like a layer of residue over the soil surface protects it from wind and rain and erosive forces, clothing our soul will do the same for us, protecting us from the temptations of the world, and helping us to keep our focus on God's ability to protect us. The tools we are to use to fully clothe ourselves, are described as "putting on the armor of God" described in Ephesians 6:

[11] **Put on the full armor of God, so that you can take your stand against the devil's schemes.** [12] **For our struggle is not against flesh and blood, but against the rulers, against the authorities, against the powers of this dark world and against the spiritual forces of evil in the heavenly realms.** [13] **Therefore put on the full armor of God, so that when the day of evil comes, you may be able to stand your ground, and after you have done everything, to stand.** [14] **Stand firm then, with the belt of truth buckled around your waist, with the breastplate of righteousness in place,** [15] **and with your feet fitted with the readiness that comes from the gospel of peace.** [16] **In addition to all this, take up the shield of faith, with which you can extinguish all the flaming arrows of the evil one.** [17] **Take the helmet of salvation and the sword of the Spirit, which is the word of God.**

There have been volumes of books written about what it means to "put on the full armor of God." But I am not aware of any that compare these instructions for protecting our soul—also as a way to manage our soil. What if we were to make that comparison—that the soul and the soil ought to be managed in the same manner? The armor described provides the means by which when bad things come, we will be able to stand firm and hold our ground—sounds like the same thing that residue can do to protect our soil from erosion. The tools mentioned above like the belt of truth, the breastplate of righteousness, the shield of faith, the helmet of salvation with the sword of the Spirit, which is the word of God, are similar in a sense to the soil health principles—using living roots and diversity as tools, and to have faith in the ability of God to do his work through His creative, regenerative forces that he gives us through His grace. It takes faith and the full use of the tools that God gives us to protect ourselves, in order to receive the full benefits of his Grace. It is describing a systems approach toward receiving His full protection and benefits. The soil heath principles can do the same thing. They describe a systematic approach to receiving the full benefits that a healthy soil can give us. Disturbances will come. Let's not create our own, and let's do everything we can to protect ourselves from destructive forces by staying the course, to not only deflect but extinguish problems. Then boldly move forward, taking an offensive posture, believing in the system that God has given to us.

14

Living Roots for the Soil

If you understand the importance of reducing disturbances in order to protect the surface of the soil, and you have adopted the practices that support those concepts, then you have taken the first steps toward improving soil health. But these two principles alone will only slow down the eventual loss of soil function. In order to restore the ability of the soil to rebuild organic matter, it takes more intensive, thoughtful management. Once the disturbances are reduced, and the soil biology can begin building soil aggregates, the biological community tends to expand. This larger and more diverse community of microbes is desirable, yet they consume a lot of food. Over time, if they are not fed, they will sort out into a community of microbes that are not functioning to their highest potential. This is quite often seen in long term no-till systems, where the soil may become hard and compacted. Even though disturbances have been reduced—the other soil health principles need to be adopted to restore the ability of the soil to work the way it is capable of working. The only way to feed microbes is to grow plants—more living roots.

Photosynthesis is how microbes are fed. Photosynthesis takes carbon and oxygen and converts it into liquid sugar called root exudates. All living plants do this in order to feed the microbial community that exists in the soil. These microbes exchange nutrients like nitrogen, phosphorus, and potassium for the carbon that is in the root exudates. This allows the microbes to be the primary source for plant nutrition.

Without the microbes, plants would need to get all their nutritional needs from whatever is dissolved in the water. This works okay if it rains, and if the water supply remains fairly steady. However, we know that is rarely the case. That is why we so often see our crops stressing out when water availability is limited. Poor water availability will reduce yield. Even in irrigated systems the amount of water required is tremendous. These systems of production—that neglect to populate a robust microbial community—require a lot of additional nutrients, that must be dissolved in water to get to the plant. Actually, it is very similar to a hydroponic system, that really does not need the soil at all.

On the other hand, maximizing the amount of time that there is a living, growing root in the soil will feed more microbes, and without disturbance they will build expansive networks that can bring the nutrient from further distances to the plant. Mycorrhizal fungi are especially adept at providing this function. AMF colonies are capable of expanding access to water in the soil profile from up to a 1,000 percent larger area. With a full complement of microbes, the plant becomes much more efficient at obtaining its needs under stressful conditions. This reduces the amount of water that is needed to keep the plant healthy under stressful conditions, because full access to the soil profile is made available.

In a way, water in the soil functions just like blood in our body. You certainly need nutrient-rich blood to stay alive, and to deliver nutrition to our cells, so that we can grow and function. In a healthy person, the volume of blood stays relatively steady. It cycles throughout our body, bringing what is needed to all our parts. If a person is in some sort of trauma and is losing blood, the most important thing to do is to stop the bleeding. Once the loss of blood is stabilized, an IV is often administered to make sure that nutrient flow to the body is maintained. It makes for an interesting comparison—Are we growing our crops by having to supply an IV, to make up for the loss of water and microbial benefits which has been brought about because of our management? How do we begin to regenerate the ability of the soil and microbial community to provide for the plant so we do not have to? It all starts with a living root.

In a healthy, undisturbed natural system, there are many plants that are providing food for the microbes through living roots for the entire duration of the growing season: Photosynthesis happening to its maximum, for as much time as possible, based on the geographic location on the planet. The sun shines. Plants are solar panels that can take its energy and turn it into something we can eat or use. Why would we ever want to limit the ability of this simple, free system? This concept then is the key to understanding a regenerative system. Matching our agricultural production systems to the environment that a natural system—in the same location—(just as it was created) can maximize the free collection of energy and allows the soil environment to have carbon stores in excess. Is it any wonder that the water cycle and the carbon cycle are broken? In the corn belt, we have largely replaced a plant community that had a living root and leaf capable of energy capture for 250-plus days a year, with one that only grows one corn or soybean crop, capturing energy for maybe, at the most, ninety days. This system of production has neglected to capture the energy from the sun for almost 75 percent of the time. Instead, we often till and leave the soil black, unprotected, and vulnerable—where the energy of the sun is evaporating the water, instead of growing a plant. This is inefficient and unsustainable. Yet this is standard practice in the corn belt. How much more production could we get if we were able to mimic more closely the natural system making use of that 75 percent rather than wasting it?

It is said in the central plains, we are always only one week away from a drought. It is critical to get timely rains, in order to get the most out of any crop. We do not have any control of the rainfall unless we are using irrigation systems. A supply of water in the soil, like blood in the body, is how nutrients are moved to the plant. So, if we only have plants growing and needing nutrients for 25 percent of the year, what happens to the water that falls during the other 75 percent?

Before we tackle that question, we need to understand something about productive soils—the type of soil we see in the corn belt that is most useful for growing high yielding crops. These soils were formed in an ecosystem, that was at one time a massive expanse of diverse, perennial grassland plants. It was grazed by millions of bison and other grassland wildlife species. Over many years, this process—of growing grass and other plants throughout the spring summer and fall growing season, and then the grass being grazed and trampled—led to a huge store of carbon in the form of organic matter in the prairie soils. The amount of annual rainfall was probably not too different than today. Think of how much water the prairie needed. The herds of buffalo probably moved to where the grass growth was lush and adequate, always moving, then leaving the area to rest and recover. So, you could say the water cycle matched the carbon cycle. They were in balance. Also, the more organic matter the soil contains, the more water it can hold. This is critically important to note.

Building organic matter is the key to having a soil that can collect and hold on to the water that falls on it. If the water cannot infiltrate, or the organic matter content is low, it will take a lot more water to grow plants. At the same time, if there are no plants, the soil can only hold so much at any one time—any excess becomes runoff. And again, if the soil is naked, exposed, and black, the water that is in the soil will be drawn toward the warmer surface through capillary action and will evaporate. This is a ridiculous and unnecessary waste of water, and opportunity. Is it any wonder, with the way we farm in the Midwest, that we are always only a week away from drought? Instead, we are always having to pray for a timely rain. Well, whose fault is it that our crops are out of water? Are we neglecting to allow the soil to accumulate and hold water to its maximum capability? What practices are we using to increase the organic matter in our soils? Those farmers that have adopted those practices have soils that are much more adept to withstanding stresses such as heat and drought. This also reduces stress and worry for the farmer as well. When you know that you have done everything you can to build organic matter and to maximize the rainfall you get, then the rest is up to God and His grace through sunshine and rainfall. You have done your part.

That is why "living roots as much as possible" is one of the soil health principles. Having living roots in the soil and green plants collecting sunshine is how organic matter is built. We need to figure out how take advantage of the other 75 percent of the water and sunshine that we receive that is outside of the normal growing season for corn and soybeans. This is the main reason and justification for using cover crops, companion crops, relay crops, inter-seeding, or any other method of getting more roots in the ground. More roots in the ground provide more leaves that act as additional solar panels to collect the free sunshine that would otherwise be wasted. They will provide additional residue and protection for the soil that will increase the water use efficiency and help keep the microbial community fed. Living roots provide the food through root exudates that will now be pumping carbon into the soil, for up to 75 percent more time out of the year. Will they use water? Yes. But without them, the water is wasted, like a bleeding wound. The energy of the sun would also be wasted, when it could have been used to grow a plant, instead of heating the soil and evaporating the water. Once this concept is embraced, the free energy and water we are blessed to receive begin to be utilized to their maximum potential. The productivity potential of the land is increased, and fertility investments into buying seed for covers and planting instead of disking becomes a very rewarding and refreshing method of farming. As the system matures, profit from the main cash crops increase, because the healthier soil begins to function as it was created, with less and less investment required from outside fertility inputs. Yields can be maintained and increased, with less money spent on fuel, chemical, and fertilizer. Why would any farmer want to reject the opportunity for those outcomes? When the concept is embraced—it becomes an "Ah-Ha" moment, and the pathway to farming with a regenerative attitude is opened. It gives a farmer the confidence to take charge of his management, making the most out of what God has given him, and trust that God is ultimately in charge of the outcome. It allows him to farm in an offensive, rather than defensive manner. It restores the soul to see the concepts work, because it displays the simplicity and brilliance of God's perfect creation.

Understanding the concepts and to change how we think about growing plants requires a leap of faith. We are taught that anything growing in our field besides the cash crop is a weed and needs to be killed, either with chemistry or tillage. A regenerative attitude is the opposite—and instead of asking "What do I need to kill today?" becomes "What can I plant and keep alive today?" Most of the reasons for rejecting the "living roots" concept lies between our ears. Do you have ears?

15

Living Roots for the Soul

The concept of keeping a living root in the soil, in order to perpetuate a vibrant, healthy microbial community is the perfect illustration of how we also should keep a living, active, and devout commitment to the management of our daily relationship with our creator. Living roots are the connection to the free gifts of the spirit. When God sent His son Jesus into the world to teach us, and to ultimately die and rise again to defeat sin, He gave us everything we need to make the most of our time here on earth. All we need to do is believe and accept this gift of salvation. Living roots are the perfect example of how to live a Christian life to its fullest potential. What are the living roots in your life?

All wisdom comes from God, and it is written down for us in the Bible. If you have never read it, how can you know what wisdom is? In Proverbs 2, the source of all wisdom is clearly defined.

My son, if you accept my words
and store up my commands within you,

²**turning your ear to wisdom**
and applying your heart to understanding—
³**indeed, if you call out for insight**
and cry aloud for understanding,
⁴**and if you look for it as for silver**
and search for it as for hidden treasure,
⁵**then you will understand the fear of the LORD**
and find the knowledge of God.
⁶**For the LORD gives wisdom;**
from his mouth come knowledge and understanding.
⁷**He holds success in store for the upright,**
he is a shield to those whose walk is blameless,
⁸**for he guards the course of the just**
and protects the way of his faithful ones.

The source of wisdom comes from the mouth of the Lord. When the Lord speaks, He uses His Word. Where is His Word written? In the Bible. What else does the Bible say about the Word of God? Listen carefully in John:

1 **In the beginning was the Word, and the Word was with God,**
and the Word was God. ²**He was with God in the**
beginning. ³**Through him all things were made; without him**
nothing was made that has been made. ⁴**In him was life, and**
that life was the light of all mankind. ⁵**The light shines in the**
darkness, and the darkness has not overcome it.

Did you hear it? In Proverbs, the Word is wisdom. Here in John, the Word was with God, and everything was created through it. The light of the world is wisdom. The Word was made flesh as the light of the world. Jesus is the Word and wisdom and the light of life. This concept is the living root we need to have in our lives, every day, as much as possible.

This light and life is free to everyone that accepts it. Again, in John chapter 3 the famous verse:

16 For God so loved the world that he gave his one and only Son, that whoever believes in him shall not perish but have eternal life.

To receive this gift—the forgiveness of your sin, and to return to your creator in eternal life—you need living roots—Jesus Christ. Jesus Christ cannot do His work in a soul that does not have life. Where do we get this life? Through His word. We are instructed to pray for wisdom, then open his word and receive it. Do you have ears? This is where you will get the living roots that help you live your Christian life to its fullest. We are to accept Jesus's living water (baptism) and His saving grace (His blood). Living roots as much as possible (reading His word) keeps us alive and under His protection, remaining in His light. In James 1 it says:

5 If any of you lacks wisdom, you should ask God, who gives generously to all without finding fault, and it will be given to you.

And in 1 Corinthians 1 is says:

30 It is because of him that you are in Christ Jesus, who has become for us wisdom from God—that is, our righteousness, holiness and redemption.

Just as plants collect light and feed the life in the soil through living roots, we as children of God are to be solar panels to collect God's Grace and feed and serve the community around us. That is the only way to keep our own lives and our communities thriving in God's light. Failure to do so allows spiritual darkness to enter. If our soul becomes lifeless, and un-protected, and prone to temptation and erosion, then other outside threats become real threats. Conversely, when times get tough, that is when the

Christian, with strong living roots, reflects the light of God's grace. Having living roots, a strong, vibrant, Christian faith is the key to building a resilient soul. It is how the organic matter of our lives is increased, and how we are led to God's calling in life for us—coming to full harvest.

Are you putting down living roots as much as possible? Is your rural church and community thriving with life and growth? Are you building organic matter or losing it? Are you comfortable just being steady and holding your own? Are outside threats having an impact? Are we leaving any areas of our soul unprotected? Are we taking full advantage of the light and rainfall that we are blessed to receive from God, or are we living defensively, continually avoiding or hiding from outside threats? Or are we living offensively and boldly, living as an example for others, and sharing the bounty of God's grace in our lives? The first step to regeneration is to make sure you have a living root in the soul as much as possible. Only then can you receive the fullest of God's benefits.

Living roots feed the soil and the soul. It is how we receive God's grace. Why would we not want to have as much as possible? Just one kind of root during just one time of year seems to be not fully utilizing the amount of light and rainfall we receive (grace). It will lead to problems with the soil (soul). How do we prevent this? With living roots (the word of God) and use of cover crops (His protection and grace). This concept is the key to regeneration of our soil (soul) and how to build organic matter (The Christian life). But there is another principle that is part of this whole idea of regeneration. Just one type of living root will not cut it. For example, do we just go to church on Sunday and forget about God's grace the rest of the week. Yes, as baptized children of God, we have a living root—but after forty or fifty years of the that same routine, we become comfortable, and one-dimensional… kind of like farming with only a two- or three-crop rotation. It will be difficult to fully experience the true benefits of regeneration.

16

Diversity in the Soil

In one teaspoon of healthy soil, there are hundreds of millions of microbes—more than people on the planet. This is not easy to conceptualize, but when you add up the total mass of the microbial community in an acre of healthy soil, it equates to the mass of two elephants. That is a lot of mouths to feed. Where does all that food come from? Primarily, it comes from carbon produced through root exudates as a result of photosynthesis. Remember, that is why it is important to have a living root as much as possible. The millions of microbes need to eat. Most of these microbes are bacteria, which can reproduce at extremely fast rates. Bacteria serve as food for other organisms that collectively form what is known as the soil food web. This includes a whole host of various fungi, protozoa, nematodes, arthropods, and earthworms. Every time one of these critters is eaten, the nutrients within are digested and expelled and become available for the plant. It is a remarkably complex system of life and death, allowing the plant to flourish. This is how plants receive their required nutrients. Plants and microbes have the ability to create their own environment called the rhizosphere, which is an area immediately around a plant root where most all of this process takes place—eating and dying, nutrient exchange, and inhaling and exhaling of oxygen. The microbial community serves the plant in the process the cycles of life and death provide the basic building block to create humus—the basic component of carbon-rich organic matter. Scientists have tried to replicate humus formation but as of yet have not been successful. Yet microbes can do it easily and have done it since they were created.

Of the millions of microbes in a healthy soil, many have been identified and their life cycle and purposes are known. For instance, it is well known that rhizobia bacteria colonize the roots of legumes and can convert nitrogen to an available form for the plant. Many, many other important plant functions are attributable to specific microbial functions. We also have become aware of the benefits of arbuscular mycorrhizal fungi networks in the soil, as mentioned before, providing access to the nutrients and water to a much larger portion of the soil environment. However, there are millions of microbes that are present, and yet we do not yet know what they do specifically. In a recent DNA analysis conducted on worm cast (poop) extract, 450 individual species of microbes were found, only 250 of which could be identified by name. Two hundred species we have not yet been named! I wonder what their function is? What important role do they play in plant nutrition and uptake? It is likely that a good share of these play a role as predators, keeping other microbes like fusarium in check. The soil food web is incredibly diverse and complex, and we have just begun to recognize its role in providing plant nutrition.

Diverse plant communities support diverse microbial communities. When we limit our plant diversity, we certainly alter the soil microbial community toward those microbes that support specific plants. Because of this simplification and monocropping management, whole communities of microbes may be missing in the soil food web. Is it any wonder why it seems we need more and more fertilizer to grow healthy crops? The microbes that are needed to supply the full nutrient needs of the plant, as well as those microbes needed for plant protection, are not present, so we as managers look for ways to make up the shortcoming. We now need to use more fungicides, pesticides, and herbicides, as well as nutrients like P and K, which are not made fully available by the microbial community anymore. This means added input costs, which will impact our profit margins. Lack of plant diversity takes us down a path of increased dependance as with our attempts to kill all the threats, we also kill the very things that might prevent the threats from becoming substantial. It is comparable to becoming addicted to drugs or painkillers. You need more and more to suppress the problem because we have not gotten to the root cause of the problem. We are just trying to address the symptoms, rather than cure the problem.

There was an experiment that was conducted on Gabe Brown's farm that has been made famous and has been replicated all over the world. It started out as a test plot to identify which species of cover crop will do best with his soils and environment. Numerous individual species were planted in strip trials side by side. Also, there was a plot that contained all the species in a mixture. A hot dry growing season basically wiped out the individual species plots, but the mixture held on and even flourished in the same conditions. What was it about the mixture that allowed it to succeed? The experiment demonstrated the power of diversity. The benefits were coming from the diverse microbial associations, allowing certain plants to provide and share nutrient resources for the whole plot. The monocultures did not have that capability, because the microbial community was too limited. This indicates that the whole is greater than the parts. This is seen in nature easily in unmanaged or uncultivated areas. During stressful times like drought, take a look around your landscape and notice where the most growth and greenery is—likely in a weed patch or shelterbelt, where a diverse plant community is present. How does that happen?

A healthy microbial population in a healthy soil can be compared to a healthy human community. Think of all the occupations that are necessary for a vibrant and robust community of people. A healthy growing community has doctors, lawyers, firemen, policemen, garbage men, grocery stores, gas stations, schools, administrators, teachers, students, pastors, congregations, recreational workers, tourist workers, industrial manufacturing, truckers, postal workers, communications workers, hospitals, nurses, clinics, restaurants, parks, trails, water treatment, sewer workers, transportation, florists, nurseries, funeral homes, laundry facilities, construction workers, real estate sales, clerks, government employees, social workers, jailors, and the list goes on and on. The microbial community must have the same level of diversity in order to function properly. If large segments of the community are missing, the community begins to have problems and begins a slow decline. If there is no school or law enforcement, other segments of the community begin to expand, and soon there are not as many jobs, and people begin to move out, or become dependent upon the government or charity. Healthy communities are always seeking jobs to keep and bring in new jobs for its people. When there is no work, there is no harvest, and God's resources are wasted or taken for granted.

Somewhere along the line, and recent in the history of agriculture, we have decided that one crop, grown under ideal conditions, with all kinds of technology and defensive traits bred into the seed, will deliver for us the maximum potential yield for that crop. Take corn for example. In the not-so-distant past, corn was crop that was grown to feed the hogs or the cattle on the farm, along with alfalfa and grass hay, to put weight gain on the animals to be sold for food and profit. As is the nature of man, we looked for ways to simplify our lives and our workload and become specialists at one or two aspects of this process. We have become extremely efficient in the production of corn and soybeans, with massive scientific advancements in seed genetics, chemical technology, planting and harvesting equipment, smart sprayers and remote technologies, and even storage and transportation to markets. One person can now produce more calories and protein per acre than ever before in history. While this may seem like the pathway to success in agriculture, the effects have been to tighten profit margins down to miniscule amounts per bushel, reduced the rural population, and enlarged the average farm acreage to an all-time high. This system of efficiency has led to having to farm more acres to make a living. Of course, government policy and risk management programs have all supported this movement. Production agriculture has become a flow chart—taking out the risk, and producing predictable, repeatable results, which the markets and credit lenders like.

Likewise, animal production for meat has also transitioned into a largely automated, production line system. Most animals are produced, fed, and finished without ever being outdoors. These efficiencies have allowed animal production to be somewhat hidden from public view and has allowed for massive expansion in the same fashion as crop production. In many cases, the animals are not even owned by the farmer, but are more or less raised under contract, paying a farmer for his buildings and labor to produce a product for delivery in certain timeframe. This is all extremely efficient and provides the consumer with a reliable, predictable, and affordable food product. There are hardly any chickens or hogs raised outdoors for production, other than on hobby farms or for 4-h projects. There is still an outdoor cow/calf ranching lifestyle, but that too is declining as more land is taken out of grass production and transitioned into grain production, that can then be fed to animals in a confinement production facility.

Although individual farm operations have become financially successful, and have expanded, it comes at the cost of others who cannot compete and must sell out or quit. Others have simply recognized that the cost of production and land has become too high, and soon the land is either sold or rented out to the highest bidder. Once the landowner is no longer on the land, management tends to be that of less diversification, removal of livestock, and more flow-chart agronomy of row-crop production. If the only market remaining is for corn and soybeans, that is what will be grown. Removal of diversification means our market and management options become limited as well.

Have we become so dependent upon agronomic systems that we have taken God out of the formula? Is your local, rural church gaining or declining? What is the average age of the folks at church attendance? Do you support one pastor for one congregation? Where is the giving coming from, and where will it come from in the future? Do the attendees give from the wealth of the land that God has blessed them to manage? How much of the land in the local community is rented? You can see why failing to remain diversified has led to unintended consequences.

These production systems have become extremely efficient, but there have been some negative social and environmental effects. As I mentioned above, the rural community is not as vibrant and robust as it once was, as fewer and fewer people are needed for labor. As a result, there are fewer people using a local café or needing groceries. Schools consolidate, as fewer families are making a living around small towns. Even local grain elevators have consolidated and can only purchase one or two grain products, as they cater to the market demand and local production practices. There are not many places where a farmer can sell flax, or barley, or even wheat or sorghum. All of this has resulted in loss of diversity in the soil, but also the community, and this has had a profoundly negative effect on the long-term viability of our agricultural systems. Science and technology have allowed us to become extremely efficient and productive, but they also have left us vulnerable to new threats and risks that require us to rethink our agricultural production practices. Diversification has always been a great way to manage those risks. Science and technology must remain tools, and not our gods. Have we become slaves to the system?

Almost every day, there is a news story about the effects of glyphosate on human health. Regardless of the science, about whether it is safe or not, the continuation of its permissible use is being threatened. Many countries (including Mexico—number one for US corn exports) are banning the use and import of glyphosate-resistant corn and soybeans. This begs the question—where in the future will we sell a crop that uses this technology? Are we able to continue our systems of production without the use of glyphosate? Does this mean we need to go back to tillage to kill weeds? What will that mean for carbon releases to the atmosphere? How are we going to keep yields up, to feed the world without the use of glyphosate? Suddenly, a new threat to our current production system and our agricultural management practices of the future needs to be reconsidered. How will you manage this on your farm? Are you ready or willing to diversify?

17

Diversity for the Soul

The Bible does have much to say about diversity. We have already mentioned the that when God created the universe, diversity was the very essence of perfection, and "It was good." Each and every microbe, plant, animal, and human were created and named. We still are unravelling the mysteries of how all of God's perfect creation is interconnected and designed to function. An appreciation for diversity includes recognition that we are part of it, and have a role to play, and it should inspire a thankful and awesome response from us. This work of the Holy Spirit is how God's grace for us leads to his harvest. God did not create a population of uniform, one-dimensional, monocropping robots to produce His harvest. Instead, He created each of us to do our part, with our talents, within our community, to His glory.

We are just like a member of a diverse plant community. We are here to collect God's light and receive His grace—in order that we will reflect His light upon others and help them grow and receive His light. No matter what we are called to do in life, this is the reason we are here. One of my favorite verses is Jeremiah 1:5:

**"Before I formed you in the womb I knew you,
before you were born I set you apart;
I appointed you as a prophet to the nations."**

God knew us by name before we were born. How awesome is that? Do you think you are here as an accident from some evolutionary process descended from apes? That thought is depressing. If evolution were fact, then survival of the fittest would require us to rid the planet of all the less-than-perfect beings. We would be able to develop a population of fully advanced, functional people, going about their programmed, flow-charted lives. We would become robots. There would be no need for love and compassion. Just exist. Unfortunately, without God, or a higher being, then only the smart people would get to decide what is just and appropriate to manage the planet and perpetuate the human species. The smart people would then become their own god—and the rest of us just work for them. This sounds like a great plan, for the demonic forces in this world to disconnect our souls from our salvation.

God created you to be you. Every skill, desire, passion, and thought that you have is yours. This is the very essence of diversity. Our differences are what make us unique, and perfectly designed to fulfill God's plan for your life. By recognizing this, embracing it, and thanking God, then asking Him to direct your decisions, it takes pressure off us. This is the peace which passes all understanding. We would like to know what God is up to, but we do not. We make plans, but they might not be God's plan. This is also a reflection of diversity. As much as we would like a risk-free, predictable future, life just doesn't always go that way. Embracing this concept and always looking for God's will in our lives will give you peace—as the outcome is His.

A description of God's grace and power over blessing our landscape is given in Psalms 65:

Praise awaits you, our God, in Zion;
to you our vows will be fulfilled.
[2] You who answer prayer,
to you all people will come.
[3] When we were overwhelmed by sins,
you forgave our transgressions.
[4] Blessed are those you choose
and bring near to live in your courts!
We are filled with the good things of your house,
of your holy temple.
[5] You answer us with awesome and righteous deeds,
God our Savior,
the hope of all the ends of the earth
and of the farthest seas,
[6] who formed the mountains by your power,
having armed yourself with strength,
[7] who stilled the roaring of the seas,
the roaring of their waves,
and the turmoil of the nations.
[8] The whole earth is filled with awe at your wonders;
where morning dawns, where evening fades,
you call forth songs of joy.
[9] You care for the land and water it;
you enrich it abundantly.
The streams of God are filled with water
to provide the people with grain,
for so you have ordained it.
[10] You drench its furrows and level its ridges;
you soften it with showers and bless its crops.
[11] You crown the year with your bounty,
and your carts overflow with abundance.
[12] The grasslands of the wilderness overflow;

the hills are clothed with gladness.
¹³ The meadows are covered with flocks
and the valleys are mantled with grain;
they shout for joy and sing.

This wonderful scripture describes the role of a Christian farmer perfectly. We are to praise God who hears us and answers our prayers. We should have a repentant heart and seek His presence. God has the power to move mountains. Access to this power is yours if you ask for and receive it. As a result, the diversity of the land will provide rich abundance for our soils and for our souls.

Another vivid description of God's power provided for us through diversity is found in Psalms 104:

¹ Praise the LORD, my soul.
LORD my God, you are very great;
you are clothed with splendor and majesty.
² The LORD wraps himself in light as with a garment;
he stretches out the heavens like a tent
³ and lays the beams of his upper chambers on their waters.
He makes the clouds his chariot
and rides on the wings of the wind.
⁴ He makes winds his messengers,
flames of fire his servants.
⁵ He set the earth on its foundations;
it can never be moved.
⁶ You covered it with the watery depths as with a garment;
the waters stood above the mountains.
⁷ But at your rebuke the waters fled,
at the sound of your thunder they took to flight;
⁸ they flowed over the mountains,
they went down into the valleys,

to the place you assigned for them.
⁹ You set a boundary they cannot cross;
never again will they cover the earth.
¹⁰ He makes springs pour water into the ravines;
it flows between the mountains.
¹¹ They give water to all the beasts of the field;
the wild donkeys quench their thirst.
¹² The birds of the sky nest by the waters;
they sing among the branches.
¹³ He waters the mountains from his upper chambers;
the land is satisfied by the fruit of his work.
¹⁴ He makes grass grow for the cattle,
and plants for people to cultivate—
bringing forth food from the earth:
¹⁵ wine that gladdens human hearts,
oil to make their faces shine,
and bread that sustains their hearts.
¹⁶ The trees of the LORD are well watered,
the cedars of Lebanon that he planted.
¹⁷ There the birds make their nests;
the stork has its home in the junipers.
¹⁸ The high mountains belong to the wild goats;
the crags are a refuge for the hyrax.
¹⁹ He made the moon to mark the seasons,
and the sun knows when to go down.
²⁰ You bring darkness, it becomes night,
and all the beasts of the forest prowl.
²¹ The lions roar for their prey
and seek their food from God.
²² The sun rises, and they steal away;
they return and lie down in their dens.

²³ Then people go out to their work,
to their labor until evening.
²⁴ How many are your works, LORD!
In wisdom you made them all;
the earth is full of your creatures.
²⁵ There is the sea, vast and spacious,
teeming with creatures beyond number—
living things both large and small.
²⁶ There the ships go to and fro,
and Leviathan, which you formed to frolic there.
²⁷ All creatures look to you
to give them their food at the proper time.
²⁸ When you give it to them,
they gather it up;
when you open your hand,
they are satisfied with good things.
²⁹ When you hide your face,
they are terrified;
when you take away their breath,
they die and return to the dust.
³⁰ When you send your Spirit,
they are created,
and you renew the face of the ground.
³¹ May the glory of the LORD endure forever;
may the LORD rejoice in his works—
³² he who looks at the earth, and it trembles,
who touches the mountains, and they smoke.
³³ I will sing to the LORD all my life;
I will sing praise to my God as long as I live.
³⁴ May my meditation be pleasing to him,
as I rejoice in the LORD.
³⁵ But may sinners vanish from the earth

and the wicked be no more.
Praise the LORD, my soul.
Praise the LORD.

God's power over creation is described here and we should be thankful and grateful for our presence in it. Even the wildlife is described as only existing and living by His hand. Again, praise and thanksgiving can be our only response to the awesomeness of His creation in all its diversity. Diversity is from God, and we should not neglect to fully embrace its power to change our soils, and our souls. Trying to simplify to maximize efficiency and production without God's direction will result in failure. Do not get trapped into thinking we have agricultural production all figured out. The diversity of creation will make us look foolish. The same is true for our faith and our soul health. Do not get comfortable. Remain steadfast and recognize that God is in charge. Pray for God's blessing on our lives, but also thank and praise Him every day for this life no matter the situation and know that we can be certain of an eternal home with our Father in heaven—because of what Christ did to redeem us. Remember, He knew us before we were born, and wants us to return home.

God also speaks to us about diversity, yet unity through the apostle Paul in 1ˢᵗ Corinthians 12:

[15] Now if the foot should say, "Because I am not a hand, I do not belong to the body," it would not for that reason stop being part of the body. [16] And if the ear should say, "Because I am not an eye, I do not belong to the body," it would not for that reason stop being part of the body. [17] If the whole body were an eye, where would the sense of hearing be? If the whole body were an ear, where would the sense of smell be? [18] But in fact God has placed the parts in the body, every one of them, just as he wanted them to be. [19] If they were all one part, where would the body be? [20] As it is, there are many parts, but one body.

21 The eye cannot say to the hand, "I don't need you!" And the head cannot say to the feet, "I don't need you!" 22 On the contrary, those parts of the body that seem to be weaker are indispensable, 23 and the parts that we think are less honorable we treat with special honor. And the parts that are unpresentable are treated with special modesty, 24 while our presentable parts need no special treatment. But God has put the body together, giving greater honor to the parts that lacked it, 25 so that there should be no division in the body, but that its parts should have equal concern for each other. 26 If one part suffers, every part suffers with it; if one part is honored, every part rejoices with it.

27 Now you are the body of Christ, and each one of you is a part of it. 28 And God has placed in the church first of all apostles, second prophets, third teachers, then miracles, then gifts of healing, of helping, of guidance, and of different kinds of tongues. 29 Are all apostles? Are all prophets? Are all teachers? Do all work miracles? 30 Do all have gifts of healing? Do all speak in tongues[d]? Do all interpret? 31 Now eagerly desire the greater gifts.

Wow! How perfectly this scripture describes how everyone has a role to play to achieve the greater gifts! How, also, it describes the earlier discussion about a diverse community. At creation, God ensured that diversity was part of the perfect picture. Imagine if God had created man without woman, leaving him without anyone to love. Imagine if God simply created the perfect garden, placed man in it, and that was it. Is there any love? Diversity allowed for free will and for true love to be expressed and displayed in the world.

Without diversity, life for mankind would be a simple-minded, monocultural, robot-like existence. What if there was no free thought or free choice? What if there was no imagination or artistic license? How would expressions of music, color, and thought ever be displayed? The diversity of humankind…races, cultures, traditions…all provide the very richness of life on earth. Removal of diversity seems to be against the fabric of creation itself.

Opposite of diversity is a monoculture. It is efficient, yet boring and predictable. Many farmers have felt this—that the art of farming is missing. The university-recommended best management practices are all good ideas, but they have taken the creativity away from the farmer and has left God out of the production equation. It can lead to feelings of emptiness and lack of joy. Farming becomes nothing but an assembly line. It leads to a work attitude of having to spray this, kill that, fix this, and buy that…always wanting more. It has been sold as the pathway to success, but it can leave one without a restful, thankful soul.

Compare this concept with how most of us now grow our crops and our food. Are there ways we could benefit our lives and the lives of those around us by including diversity in our production systems? Certainly, more diversity could be included in our crop rotations. The soil and the microbes that live there would certainly benefit. So would our long-term yields and ability to fend off weeds and pests. We have already discussed how it is important to fill the growing season with green growth and protect the soil surface. Adding a cover crop is a great way to start down the regenerative path. Watching the growth of a cover crop and understanding the concepts as to why you do it can be some of the most rewarding and educational practices that you can do on your farm. The whole exercise, when framed around the idea that you are collecting free energy that is otherwise wasted, changes your attitude about using them. When the concept is embraced, true regenerative processes begin to occur, and the results really start to pay off. At this point, you obtain an attitude that appreciates the unseen life in the soil, and a desire is developed to nurture and care for it—fostering more life. This will allow you to farm in a proactive manner, rather than a reactive manner—eliminating problems before they start, rather than conducting all kinds of remedial actions. It is very rewarding to see your intentional efforts result in successful outcomes.

Not to say that cover crops are the "be all, end all" answer to all problems—there will always be thorns and thistles—but they do bring a whole new set of management options for you that will diversify the life in your soil and promote an exciting, exploratory opportunity to learn something new about plant and soil interactions. Intentionally managing for more diversity will provide opportunities to experience joy, appreciation, and wonder about God's creation and how it works. To witness an increase in water infiltration or notice an improvement in soil structure brings confidence and purpose for using cover crops and verifies that you are on a beneficial path. The invisible community of microbes, and the power of the work that they can do start to become very visible. This is regenerative for your soul.

There are simple joys in seeing the wildlife, including insects and plants, flourish in a diverse environment. These things need places to exist. If we manage every acre for maximum corn production every year, where will they live? When they have moved on or simply are gone, where will those simple pleasures be found? Large landscapes already are completely void of wildlife diversity. It is one of the first indications of a broken carbon and water cycle—wildlife will move out. It may take a few years, but next to go are the people. Has the school consolidated in your community? Has your rural church formed a dual or tri-parish, or closed completely? Is this how we want to live in our rural environment? What will it take to reverse these trends? It takes the full richness of diversity to achieve mutually beneficial outcomes. This happens in the soil—and it happens in our soul. It may be time for some deep soul-searching. "Do you have ears?"

The apostle Paul taught about our role in advancing God's kingdom in 1st Corinthians 3:

> [5] **What, after all, is Apollos? And what is Paul? Only servants, through whom you came to believe—as the Lord has assigned to each his task. [6] I planted the seed, Apollos watered it, but**

God has been making it grow. ⁷ So neither the one who plants nor the one who waters is anything, but only God, who makes things grow. ⁸ The one who plants and the one who waters have one purpose, and they will each be rewarded according to their own labor. ⁹ For we are co-workers in God's service; you are God's field, God's building.

¹⁰ By the grace God has given me, I laid a foundation as a wise builder, and someone else is building on it. But each one should build with care. ¹¹ For no one can lay any foundation other than the one already laid, which is Jesus Christ.

Paul compares the growth of our spiritual life to that of what happens to a seed that has been planted. The Holy Spirit uses us to bring ourselves and others into a relationship with Him. Consider yourself a farmer of God's grace, given to us through Jesus, the foundation of our faith. There are various roles for each of us, but none of it happens without God's help, which He promises to give us if we ask. It makes one wonder, really, is our identity as a farmer really about corn and soybeans at all? How we live our lives and manage our farm is a perfect picture of how God's field, or kingdom is built.

Jesus also described God's kingdom in His parable of the growing seed in Mark 4:

²⁶ He also said, "This is what the kingdom of God is like. A man scatters seed on the ground. ²⁷ Night and day, whether he sleeps or gets up, the seed sprouts and grows, though he does not know how. ²⁸ All by itself the soil produces grain—first the stalk, then the head, then the full kernel in the head. ²⁹ As soon as the grain is ripe, he puts the sickle to it, because the harvest has come."

³⁰ Again he said, "What shall we say the kingdom of God is like, or what parable shall we use to describe it? ³¹ It is like a mustard seed, which is the smallest of all seeds on earth. ³² Yet when planted, it grows and becomes the largest of all garden plants, with such big branches that the birds can perch in its shade."

What a beautiful description of a Christian life, describing the word of God as a tiny mustard seed, growing and maturing into a comforting place for rest and peace. Again, it is the work of the Holy Spirit, to turn that seed—the Word—Jesus Christ, into a fully mature and useful farmer for God's harvest.

18

Animals on the Land

Animals on our land, both cropland and pasture, are one of the best ways to bring diversity into a system to improve soil health. Under proper management, animal grazing can really accelerate the speed at which the benefits from that diversity can be obtained. First of all, grazing animals can cycle crop residue and cover crop resources and quite efficiently return those nutrients back to soil where they came from. If you think about it, back to the formula for photosynthesis, carbon as a gas is taken out of the atmosphere, liquified, and converted into a solid as plant material. The plant grows and matures, where it provides a seed harvest, and the residue is left behind. When a grazing animal eats a portion of that residue, and tramples another good portion, the biological community is fed, and that carbon now has the chance to be converted into humus, the materials used for building the structures for that biological community to thrive. Animals become an important part of the system. This is how the natural, created system has always worked. Removing animals from the system will slow it down. Removing the residue from that field will slow it even further, as a shortage of carbon for the microbial community will reduce its potential to build its community. This is often the difference between building organic matter in the soil or losing it.

Crop residues and pasture grasses that have been left in the field can be grazed well after the growing season. These "stockpiled" resources become another way to really ramp up a carbon-building rather than a carbon-depleting management approach. Instead of making hay and moving the carbon and other nutrients to the animals to feed them in a different location, feed stocks are left in the field, and animals are brought to them. This type of management keeps all the nutrients and associated microbial functions going in the field where the plants were grown, allowing those soils to keep the benefits of the rain and sunshine in place. Animals cycle those resources by grazing and defecating in the same field cycling those nutrients even—through the winter months—in their warm, microbe-rich rumen. This extends and speeds up the cycling of the nutrients in fields that otherwise would have nothing going on, with respect toward decomposition, until spring warm up. This change in management system has resulted in tremendous gains in soil carbon, and has improved the economics of the operation, as not nearly as much time and energy are expended on haying, baling or stacking, moving, and feeding of the feed materials. Also, instead of having to replace those nutrients, by spreading manure or purchasing off-farm fertilizer, the animals recycle them in place. For these reasons, animals can then become one of the best tools we have to manage the organic matter content in our soil. Also, animals that are grazed through the winter seem to be healthier and more content. Winter grazing does present its challenges—such as freezing water, and deep snow and ice situations, but good managers have found all kinds of innovative ways to manage those issues, such as using bale grazing, electric fence, and in-ground, or solar-heated water sources.

Animals on the land can also bring opportunities for stacking enterprises, such as following the cattle with chickens, or grazing hogs. Every animal has different feeding and foraging habits that bring diversity of the microbial community back into play. The nutrient content of the manure of these animals become source for many of the macro and micros that the soil needs to supply future crops. Stacking enterprises if conducted with the intent to build soil organic matter, can really improve soil biology and speed up recovery of soil health and water and nutrient cycles.

Animals bring an important increased level of biological diversity that is not always apparent. The hair, saliva, urine, mucous, and even afterbirth bring a community of microbes that function in the soil web system to the benefit of the larger community. The complexities of all these benefits are just beginning to be studied. Suffice it know that the natural system included a diverse community of animals—including wild ones—that are important to the overall function of the community. Removal of that diversity reduces the opportunity to provide soil benefits of which we may not even be aware.

Animals also can provide an additional source of income, as they are a way to convert God's free sunshine and rainfall into protein. There is an additional level of management associated with that opportunity, but when you look at animals as management tools for God's free resources, you realize how much opportunity we really have in order to benefit from those gifts. Animals become gifts as well—not simply dollars and more work.

Incorporating animals back on the land helps to bring a proper attitude for the management of our plant and animal resources. It all is only possible with God's gifts and our job it to manage those gifts to His glory—not exploit them for our own selfish purposes. This proper attitude is important for our own mental health, as every day we are given the opportunity to be managers in God's kingdom and enjoy the benefits of His love for us. Work then becomes less stressful when we realize that God has had enough confidence in us to place us in this high-level management position. Ask Him for help, thank him for the job, and just see if work becomes a little more fun. This can go a long way toward improving the health of our soul as well. God promises to provide us with everything we need when we recognize Him. Jesus said in Matthew 6:

[25]"*Therefore I tell you, do not worry about your life, what you will eat or drink; or about your body, what you will wear. Is not life more than food, and the body more than clothes?* [26]*Look at the birds of the air; they do not sow or reap or store away in barns, and yet your heavenly Father feeds them. Are you not much more valuable than they?* [27]*Can any one of you by worrying add a single hour to your life?* [28]*"And why do you worry about clothes? See how the flowers of the field grow. They do not labor or spin.* [29]*Yet I tell you that not even Solomon in all his splendor was dressed like one of these.* [30]*If that is how God clothes the grass of the field, which is here today and tomorrow is thrown into the fire, will he not much more clothe you-you of little faith?* [31]*So do not worry, saying, 'What shall we eat?' or 'What shall we drink?' or 'What shall we wear?'* [32]*For the pagans run after all these things, and your heavenly Father knows that you need them.* [33]*But seek first his kingdom and his righteousness, and all these things will be given to you as well.* [34]*Therefore do not worry about tomorrow, for tomorrow will worry about itself. Each day has enough trouble of its own.*

This is one of the most comforting verses in the Bible. When we are feeling stressed out about our farm or ranch operation, due to things beyond our control such as the weather, prices, policy, or regulation, maybe it is time to stop, take a good look at what God has provided, thank Him, and ask for help. Then, to God's glory, explore adopting concepts of management that potentially could improve your soil carbon, through recognition and management of the unseen microbial community that lives in the soil. Feeding this invisible community is how we feed our own soul and is a great way to reconnect with God's grace. Then, leave it to Him. Go forward with faith and confidence. The effects on your soil, and your soul, will be profound. "Do you have ears?"

19

Salt and Light

As we discussed earlier, productive farmland that begins to suffer from saline conditions can only be remediated with a change in management and mindset. All lands are not created equal, and every soil can only produce to its certain inherent capability. Our job as farmer or landowner is to protect and manage that soil to its maximum capability. Sometimes this may mean that a certain soil in a certain environment simply cannot sustainably produce under annual row crop production, unless very specific carbon-conscious practices are maintained. Remember, bare soil is extremely vulnerable to many threats. Bare soil promotes evaporation, and water that evaporates leaves behind its dissolved solids—often those are salts.

Salts are a very necessary part of a healthy, functioning soil ecosystem. Salts provide the basic nutrient bank that microbes need, and then ultimately allow those nutrient-rich compounds to be accessible for plant uptake. In healthy soil, arbuscular mycorrhizal fungi bring those nutrients to the plant through their extensive networks that are built up in the soil allowing the plant to communicate its nutrient needs, and the fungi go and get it, bringing it to the plant root, and exchange it for carbon. It is a beautiful system and an example of a symbiotic relationship, where both the plant and the fungi work together to build and maintain a healthy environment in which they both can thrive.

Management plays a large role in keeping this system functioning. Of course, tillage and low diversity eliminate the presence of these vast underground networks. Without them, plants must be provided access to all these nutrients in a different manner. The plant becomes much more dependent upon timely rainfall to provide access to these dissolved nutrients. What if it does not rain? In the absence of the fungi, the plant begins to show nutrient deficiencies and drought stress. So, is it a lack of rainfall, too much rainfall, or poor management that is the cause of a worsening salinity problem? If not dealt with early, it begins to worsen. Eventually it can get to the point where the soil particle charge becomes positively charged—and like charges repel. This causes soil aggregates to completely fall apart—called dispersion. This situation is almost impossible to recover from, and over time, these areas become like deserts. Without plants, the soil completely loses its ability to function.

Salinity is a huge indicator of a problem. It shows the need for a correction. It takes time to cause salinity, and it takes time to fix salinity—but ignorance will not solve the problem. There are various management options, but likely the best fix is to let the plants grow and recover the microbial community associated with it. Early successional annual plants will establish first—often what we call weeds—but they are the first step to recovery. Eventually, deep-rotted perennial vegetation will establish and begin to fix the soil structure and begin to restore a functional water cycle. Only then can these areas provide a return on investment and begin to recover—providing a useful value back to the tenant.

Jesus spoke about this in Luke 6:

6 Then he told this parable: "A man had a fig tree growing in his vine-

yard, and he went to look for fruit on it but did not find any. ⁷ So he said to the man who took care of the vineyard, 'For three years now I've been coming to look for fruit on this fig tree and haven't found any. Cut it down! Why should it use up the soil?'

⁸ "'Sir,' the man replied, 'leave it alone for one more year, and I'll dig around it and fertilize it. ⁹ If it bears fruit next year, fine! If not, then cut it down.'"

The fertilizer of the day was likely manure, but no matter the content, the point is the tree was given more time, and some salt. Compare this with our relationship with our Lord and savior Jesus Christ. Are we waiting for the right time to fully accept his saving grace and express that relationship in how we live? How much time do we have? Is God going to be patient with this world forever? Are we producing figs, or just taking up soil? Maybe reading this parable with that frame of reference will provide a little salt for you?

In the Bible, salt is used to describe our relationship with God. God defines how salt is to be viewed in our lives. In Luke 14 Jesus speaks directly about salt:

³⁴ "Salt is good, but if it loses its saltiness, how can it be made salty again? ³⁵ It is fit neither for the soil nor for the manure pile; it is thrown out.

"Whoever has ears to hear, let them hear."

Jesus had just spoke several parables to the Pharisees about common sense, humility, self-awareness, and the nature of humankind to calculate the cost of being a Christian. These are hard sayings. Jesus did not mince his words when he said we would have to give up everything we have in order to follow him. He then asks the salt question. Remember He is speaking to the Pharisees, who will eventually send Him to the cross. He is talking about our faith and what it means to follow him. Salt is good, as it is used to season for taste, and cure and preserve, but once it is used up, it is worthless. He is talking about our devotion to the Christian life. He is not interested in lukewarm, feel-good, believe-in-me-only-when-it-is-comfortable-type followers. This type of believer will reject him when the going gets tough. This is like salt that has lost its saltiness—a pathway to Hell. (Remember how Lot's wife looked back to Sodom and turned into a pillar of salt? Gen. 19:26) Rather we are to reject the devil and his schemes, hold firm, and renounce any sort of worship, other than Christ crucified for our sins. Those type of believers are "the salt of the earth."

In Matthew 5, Jesus speaks the beatitudes. Jesus is talking about who will inherit the kingdom of heaven. It worth reading again:

He said:

> [3] *"Blessed are the poor in spirit,*
> *for theirs is the kingdom of heaven.*
> [4] *Blessed are those who mourn,*
> *for they will be comforted.*
> [5] *Blessed are the meek,*
> *for they will inherit the earth.*
> [6] *Blessed are those who hunger and thirst for righteousness,*
> *for they will be filled.*
> [7] *Blessed are the merciful,*
> *for they will be shown mercy.*
> [8] *Blessed are the pure in heart,*
> *for they will see God.*
> [9] *Blessed are the peacemakers,*
> *for they will be called children of God.*
> [10] *Blessed are those who are persecuted because of righteousness,*
> *for theirs is the kingdom of heaven.*
> [11] *"Blessed are you when people insult you, persecute you and falsely say all kinds of evil against you because of me. [12] Rejoice and be glad, because great is your reward in heaven, for in the same way they persecuted the prophets who were before you.*

Then immediately following those words, He says this:

13 "You are the salt of the earth. But if the salt loses its saltiness, how can it be made salty again? It is no longer good for anything, except to be thrown out and trampled underfoot.

14 "You are the light of the world. A town built on a hill cannot be hidden. 15 Neither do people light a lamp and put it under a bowl. Instead, they put it on its stand, and it gives light to everyone in the house. 16 In the same way, let your light shine before others, that they may see your good deeds and glorify your Father in heaven.

Jesus spells out clearly here, that our faith in Him is compared to salt and light. If you are a committed Christian, it is a devotion that may cost you every comfort you have in this earthly life. Denying him is the unforgivable sin. Instead, we should reflect the light of Christ in our lives for others to see. Our words and actions should exemplify a lifestyle reflective of that faith, to God's glory. This is how the gospel of Jesus Christ through the work of the Holy Spirit is expressed. On the other hand, hiding the fact that we are Christian does no one else any good. It is like salt that has lost its saltiness. It is good for nothing.

As a Christian farmer, how we manage our land should be based on the basic scientific fact that sunlight is the source of all growth and provides all the energy for everything we grow and produce. Our management practices should show that we are using that light to its fullest potential. Not recognizing or appreciating that sunlight is the source of our existence can lead to practices that waste our potential. Conversely, capturing every bit of sunlight that we can through living plants is how soil is kept healthy and functioning. Every day, we should look upon the sunlight as a blessing from God—a gift of His grace. Sunlight provides the light of this world, just as Jesus Christ's life is given for you—for free! Use it—don't waste it. "Do you have ears?"

20

Water

As we discussed in the early chapters on creation, remember water was present as we read in Genesis 1:2.

> **² Now the earth was formless and empty, darkness was over the surface of the deep, and the Spirit of God was hovering over the waters.**

It seems to describe a situation our human minds will have a hard time understanding but it seems that water was present with God at the beginning. Water must be present to create life. There is still so much we do not fully understand about water.

Water has some very peculiar physical characteristics. Most liquids, when cooled toward turning into a solid, become denser. Not so with water. Water becomes less dense, as its molecules spread apart to form ice. That is why ice cubes float—liquid water is denser than ice. This is unique to water and thankfully so, or the waters in our lakes in the wintertime in the northerly latitudes would freeze from the bottom up. That would not work out very well for fish!

Another characteristic of water, that is a bit more on the cutting edge of current scientific exploration, is the ability of water, in the presence of infrared energy (which comes from sunlight by the way), to separate its molecules into an organized pattern that creates an electrical charge. This little understood characteristic has the potential to completely change how we think about how plants take up nutrients and how by staying hydrated, the cells in our body function. Check out a book titled *The Fourth Phase of Water* by Professor Gerald H. Pollack. In this book, Dr. Pollack describes this characteristic of water that we are just beginning to understand that will shed new light on the principles of agriculture, medicine, and energy as we currently understand them. Water may very well be the key to a regenerative future.

Farmers and gardeners know very well the difference between water that comes from natural rainfall and water that comes out of a pipe or hose. Plants respond in a whole different manner to natural rainfall from the heavens. As far as I know, no real substantive evidence has ever proven why that is. Could it be that water in the form of rainfall has an electrical characteristic that allows nutrients and plant root uptake to work in a much more efficient manner? And what about microbial responses to that water? Could it be that as the plant takes in that water and its nutrients, that the plant is able to respond with an output of specific chemical signals in its root exudates, that trigger a reproductive stimulus to beneficial microbes? These are questions that are being researched that potentially can turn our current understanding of plant nutrition and the need for fertilizers on its head. As more and more of these theories are explored by science, the more we can see God's system that He created at work.

The term "quorum sensing" describes a process by which microbes detect each other's presence to see if they are there in enough numbers to turn on genes that function toward a specific outcome. There is a constant battle going on at the microbial level between good microbes and bad microbes, and in healthy systems, good guys usually win. But in compromised systems, often due to some outside influence, sometimes the bad guys show up, and do bad things. This is the case seen with many fungal or bacterial plant diseases. Something physically, chemically, or environmentally has given the bad guys an advantage. Could it be chlorine in the water, or some sort of fungicide or seed treatment that reduces the number of good guys that should be present to keep the bad guys in check? There is so much yet to learn about our production practices, and the unknown effects they may be having on microbial health.

Recent research has indicated that there may be beneficial microbes in rainwater that benefit plants on the leaf surface. If the plant is in a healthy state, plants may be able to obtain nitrogen through these free-living nitrogen fixing microbes. There is more research being conducted, working to expand that concept, to see if those processes can be triggered through application of compost extracts, and other foliar applications such as fish hydrolysates. The work is fascinating and holds tremendous potential for farmers to reduce their dependance upon commercial fertilizer and fungicides. However, at the field level results have been so variable and unpredictable that these techniques have not been fully adopted to scale across the agricultural landscape. It takes a certain amount of curiosity and a willingness to step outside of the norm for a farmer to take valuable land and experiment with these practices. It also takes a faithful attitude and belief that the concepts will work. It is understandable. Production agriculture has given us some time-tested, proven practices that have given us successful yields and outcomes, but at what price?

One must ask, was it by God's design and plan that by using fertilizers and chemicals, we reduce the health of our water? Is it okay to just keep poisoning our wells and our rivers with too much nitrogen and phosphorus? Is this just an acceptable byproduct of what we must do to grow corn and soybeans to feed the world? Or are there better ways? Are there things you can do on your farm that reduce the potential for bad things to get into our soil and water? Can we reduce how much fertilizer we need, and still produce equal or even better yields? Can we reduce how much we must spend on inputs? One thing is certain: input costs are not going to get cheaper. Input costs are always going to go up over time, especially as the cost of energy and transportation rise. Why would anyone allow nutrients and water to flow downstream, without getting paid for them? Is this treadmill of increased costs, time, energy, and all the stress that comes with it God's plan? How we use our water and the condition of the water that does leave our farm are good indicators of our soil health. Managing for better soil health means better use of the life-giving water that we get for free from our Father in heaven. Water is a blessing, not a curse, but it depends on how you use it. In Isaiah 55:

As the rain and the snow

come down from heaven,

and do not return to it

without watering the earth

and making it bud and flourish,

so that it yields seed for the sower and bread for the eater,

¹¹ so is my word that goes out from my mouth:

It will not return to me empty,

but will accomplish what I desire

and achieve the purpose for which I sent it.

And in Matthew 5, as he records the words of Jesus given in His sermon on the mount, He said:

⁴⁵ that you may be children of your Father in heaven. He causes his sun to rise on the evil and the good, and sends rain on the righteous and the unrighteous.

Water is a critical component of life on earth, as well as for living a life with Christ through the sacrament of Holy Baptism. Through Baptism, water and the Word provide a welcomed acceptance into God's family and provide the foundation for living a Christian life and death, believing that Christ had wiped our sins clean with the shedding of His blood on the cross, providing grace for us from the Father, through His Son Jesus Christ—free to all who accept him and are baptized into His Kingdom.

Pray that the Holy Spirit inspires in us a desire to learn how to best use His gifts, not for our own glory, but for His! Cool, clean, refreshing water to quench our own thirst is the result.

21

Another Fig Tree

A very interesting thing happened during the events of Holy Week, the days leading up to Jesus's crucifixion and resurrection. The small event is easily overshadowed by the grand Palm Sunday entrance, the last supper, the events leading to Jesus's arrest at the garden of Gethsemane and his trial. But look at Mark 11:

¹² The next day as they were leaving Bethany, Jesus was hungry. ¹³ Seeing in the distance a fig tree in leaf, he went to find out if it had any fruit. When he reached it, he found nothing but leaves, because it was not the season for figs. ¹⁴ Then he said to the tree,

"May no one ever eat fruit from you again."

And his disciples heard him say it.

From there, Jesus overturned the tables of the moneychangers in the temple, causing all kinds of concern amongst the faith leaders of the day. Jesus was not hiding who He was, or what the purpose of His appearance in Jerusalem was all about.

Picking up in Mark 11:

²⁰ In the morning, as they went along, they saw the fig tree withered from the roots. ²¹ Peter remembered and said to Jesus, "Rabbi, look! The fig tree you cursed has withered!"

²² "Have faith in God," Jesus answered. ²³ "Truly] I tell you, if anyone says to this mountain, 'Go, throw yourself into the sea,' and does not doubt in their heart but believes that what they say will happen, it will be done for them. ²⁴ Therefore I tell you, whatever you ask for in prayer, believe that you have received it, and it will be yours. ²⁵ And when you stand praying, if you hold anything against anyone, forgive them, so that your Father in heaven may forgive you your sins."

Now we have already discussed Jesus's parable about the fig tree that needed a bit of fertilizer and more time. This fig tree on the other hand was a real tree, not a parable, cursed by our Lord, and it withered and died overnight! No fertilizer for this tree. It was not even the season for figs to be ripe, yet life was over for this tree. What was all of this about? Yes, Jesus explained right after this that the power of prayer is strong enough to move mountains, overcoming all of nature and scientific explanation. He also directs His disciples to be pure of heart, and their prayers will be answered. But what about that poor tree? In Matthew 24, Jesus says,

³² "Now learn this lesson from the fig tree: As soon as its twigs get tender and its leaves come out, you know that summer is near. ³³ Even so, when you see all these things, you know that it is near, right at the door.

This statement is made in Matthew 24, where Jesus is clearly speaking about events leading up to the end times. He is giving His disciples words of encouragement, that we still have today—His words will not pass away (Matt. 24:35). The first fig tree is given more time to produce, but this fig tree produced no fruit—even though it was not time.

The parable of the fig tree is not so much about the tree but is more about the fruit that it is capable of producing. We do not know when we are going to die. We might live to see the end times, or we might die tomorrow of a car crash or have a heart attack. Have we produced any fruit? When is it the right season? What are you waiting for? Do you have ears to hear?

Jesus spoke about a very successful farmer in Luke 12:

16 And he told them this parable: "The ground of a certain rich man yielded an abundant harvest. 17 He thought to himself, 'What shall I do? I have no place to store my crops.'
18 "Then he said, 'This is what I'll do. I will tear down my barns and build bigger ones, and there I will store my surplus grain. 19 And I'll say to myself, "You have plenty of grain laid up for many years. Take life easy; eat, drink and be merry."'
20 "But God said to him, 'You fool! This very night your life will be demanded from you. Then who will get what you have prepared for yourself?'
21 "This is how it will be with whoever stores up things for themselves but is not rich toward God.

The gospel of Jesus Christ is that He has died for our sins, and we have free access to this gift. We are to live—and farm with that joy in our hearts. The fruit we produce is fully dependent upon that truth. Science and technology are there to support that concept, not replace it. You cannot expect to produce a useful harvest or fruit if you are only doing so for your own selfish intent. Yet with a faithful and thankful attitude, management that reflects those values will produce fruit far beyond the farm gate. If you are truly going to help feed the world, it will take much more than simply overflowing bushels. Spreading the gospel and bringing others to Christ is the real fruit of the Christian life, and that will bring you joy and peace beyond all understanding. In Matthew 7, Jesus said:

[15] "Beware of false prophets, who come to you in sheep's clothing, but inwardly they are ravenous wolves. [16] You will know them by their fruits. Do men gather grapes from thornbushes or figs from thistles? [17] Even so, every good tree bears good fruit, but a bad tree bears bad fruit. [18] A good tree cannot bear bad fruit, nor can a bad tree bear good fruit. [19] Every tree that does not bear good fruit is cut down and thrown into the fire. [20] Therefore by their fruits you will know them.

What do the fruits of your labor show others about what is in your heart? Are you as Christian farmer farming with a full appreciation and attitude of providing healthy produce that others will eat and be sustained? Would you eat your own fruit, knowing it was produced under God's watchful eye using His pro-life, creative system of growth? The fruits of your labor can be the way you can show others that you truly care about them, and they can see what is in your heart. Your production practices become regenerative for others that support and appreciate what you are doing. Rather than striving for maximum efficiency and big yields, a regenerative approach looks to obtain highest quality first, and then even bigger yields—yields we may not even be able to see or count, yields of a hundred-fold, produced from the good soil.

22

Regeneration

There is an interesting comparison between healthy soil and a healthy human. This was illustrated to me in an unpleasant manner, as I witnessed my father, whose kidneys had failed, discontinue dialysis, which he had been subject to twice a week for three years. Modern medicine can do amazing things, keeping loved ones alive and comfortable for as long as possible, but in Dad's case, he had developed a bacterial infection on a heart value that simply could not be beaten. The decision was made to discontinue dialysis at that time. His death was inevitable. But in that period over the course of several weeks, he was kept comfortable with combinations of drugs and intravenous medications. He did not eat much, because all his comfort was being supplied artificially. In an odd sort of way, it stuck me that this is how hydroponic production works. Everything the plant needs nutritionally is supplied by nutrients dissolved in water, and the plant is incapable of surviving upon its removal.

Contrast this with a healthy human, with fully healthy functioning systems—who does not need any artificial means of life support. Healthy humans eat, drink water, inhale and exhale, digest, export waste, and generate energy for work, all without any artificial assistance. Healthy plants should function the same way in a healthy soil. We should not need to supply a whole bunch of nutrients and drugs to keep plants healthy. Plants do need water and adequate nutrition, and if conditions are less than ideal, plants will begin to indicate stress. Modern agriculture has systematically, much like the pharmaceutical industry, developed all kinds of remedial drugs and medications to relieve plant stress. All these things have an impact in the soil at the microbial level. The chemicals and fertilizer we choose to use will select and favor distinct microbes and eliminate others. Eventually, we end up with a soil that is missing the very microbes that are necessary for providing plant nutrition, and we must provide those nutrients artificially. In a sense, we created our own problem, the result of which is a plant that is dependent upon additional inputs. This is no different than a human that is hooked or dependent on drugs. To solve these issues, we need to get to the root cause. We need to ask, "Why are my plants susceptible to pests and disease?" Is that just the way it is, or have I done something to my plants or soils that have limited its defense mechanisms? Just like a healthy person likely lives a healthy lifestyle, with a balanced diet and exercise, so, too, do the microbes in the soil need a healthy diet and exercise. There are no magic pills or shortcuts.

Our spiritual health—which is more important than our physical health—also needs a regular diet and exercise. Just like the soil microbiome, which God created, can be easily neglected, or forgotten, our relationship with our Father in Heaven and the advantages available to us through His grace given through the death of His son on the cross can become distant or inconvenient for our lifestyle. We all sin. You cannot be good enough to earn salvation. You also cannot be too sinful to be saved. The key is to accept God's grace. Quit beating yourself up for being sinful and quit neglecting to receive and accept God's forgiveness when you do.

God's plan of forgiveness for us is a system of plenty or excess. You have everything you need to live a healthy, productive, content spiritual life here on earth. It is clearly exemplified by God's creation that produces life on earth. It, too, is a system of excess. Consider these comparisons:

Sunlight = God's energy (Christ)

Rainfall = Life-giving transportation (blood)

Carbon and Nitrogen = Grace and forgiveness - blessings obtained through Christ

Microbes = Faith - that must be fed

Nutrients = Available with Faith

Soil = Soul (Eternal life in heaven…or Hell)

Is there any part of this system that is lacking? Can we do anything to change the fact that Christ died for us? If grace upon grace is given to us through sunlight and rainfall, why wouldn't we want to receive and accept all we can get? Why wouldn't we want to maximize their use? Why wouldn't we want to grow our faith and deepen our understanding of God's system of regeneration? The results are good fruit, yielding a hundredfold, in this life on earth. It also gives us eternal life with our Father— our creator—in heaven. That is the true outcome of God's system of regeneration, given to us through Christ's death and resurrection. That is how we truly regenerate our soul and restore a perfect relationship with our Father. All you need to do is accept it. You have the choice. Do you have ears?

23

Sustainability Under the Law and Gospel

Farm Bills: The 1977 and 1990 "Farm Bills" describe sustainable agriculture as an integrated system of plant and animal production practices having a site-specific application that will, over the long term:

+ satisfy human food and fiber needs;
+ enhance environmental quality and the natural resource base upon which the agricultural economy depends;
+ make the most efficient use of nonrenewable resources and on-farm resources and integrate, where appropriate, natural biological cycles and controls;
+ sustain the economic viability of farm operations; and
+ enhance the quality of life for farmers and society as a whole.

Sustainability definitions for agriculture generally include three aspects that must be considered, or conditions that must be met to a satisfactory level to provide societal benefits including safe and nutritious food, protection of the environment, and provision of a profitable return from its production. For something to be labelled sustainable, all three conditions must be met. These conditions must be maintained for the long haul, over the course of generations. Is production agriculture today sustainable? Is your farm sustainable? It depends upon your perspective.

There are 13,600,000 pounds of phosphorus on a unit train of soybeans. If those soybeans are going to a destination outside of the country, how are we going to get that phosphorus back onto the land to continue production? How many years can we do this? Is this sustainable?

1.6 million metric tons of nitrogen are entering the Gulf of Mexico each year from the Mississippi River Basin. Is this acceptable? What if you are a fisherman or shrimper dependent upon a fresh supply of ocean-sourced protein for your income? What happens to the diversity of the ocean fishery if the oxygen is depleted from the enlarging "dead zone" in the Gulf? Is this sustainable?

The concentration of CO2 in the atmosphere has reached a new high level of 416 ppm. Is this sustainable? We really do not know the full extent of the effects this will have on agriculture. At the same time, we are contributing nitrous oxide and methane to the atmosphere at an all-time high as well. Actually, the "greenhouse gas" that is having the most impact on agricultural production and climate is likely water vapor. There is less liquid fresh water on the planet, and more in the form of water vapor than ever before. What impact will this have on global food supplies? Is this sustainable?

We have some serious issues to confront if we expect to feed a growing population on this planet. UN estimates peg the world population to increase by eighty-three million per year. How are these challenges going to be met? Do you feel a responsibility to manage your farm in a fashion that can achieve every one of these sustainability defined outcomes? Plus, you still need to make a living and provide for your own family. The responsibility is overwhelming. How are we to manage all these sustainability demands?

No matter how you are managing your farm today, or how you choose to do it in the future, it will not matter if you are not managing it for God's glory. Today, there is a wealth of information about soil health and sustainable management, easily obtainable with just few clicks on your cell phone. Best practice information is no longer dependent upon a university research paper, waiting to be published and communicated to farmers through extension services. Communication is happening at record speed, with information about new practices and concepts being suggested and sold faster than ever before. Many false prophets are lurking in this space. It is more difficult than ever to sort it all out, and it can be intimidating to entertain new agronomic concepts that challenge our conventional beliefs about farming. At the same time, considerable evidence is mounting by early adopter-farmers that if we manage for soil health, many other benefits will follow. As such, soil health advocacy and policies are developing that encourage a shift toward these concepts. Use caution, and a critical mind. In fact, if you attend a conference or workshop promoting soil health, it will remind you very much of a religious revival, with testimony from farm managers that "have seen the light." Make sure you are well versed in the truth of creation before you accept any of these self-preservation concepts. You need to use biblical wisdom to develop your attitude and beliefs about agriculture.

First of all, you must accept the truth that all the earth was created toward your benefit as a blessing for you. Secondly, you must recognize that you are not the owner but only a temporary manager in His creation. Thirdly, before you can ever begin to tackle issues such as sustainability, you must thank and praise the Lord for your position as caretaker. Then ask Him for help. Faith in Christ will provide the pathway toward regeneration.

The only truly sustainable outcome that will be produced from this earth is a life centered around the saving grace of our Lord and Savior Jesus Christ. This is spiritual sustainability. You cannot begin to achieve sustainable outcomes in this physical world without that basis for decision-making. We can come up with all kinds of schemes to incentivize sustainable farming behavior, but at the end of the day, we are all going to die. Some may suffer. Some may die by premature or violent means. Some may die uncomfortably or in hunger. Some may die peacefully after a long life—never having want of anything. The outcome is still the same—death. Does the accumulation of land and wealth and resources matter at that point? What will become of all the wealth? Who will be the next caretaker of your land? Will the land still be managed to provide a blessing for others, or will it become just a source of rental income for disconnected owners? When it comes to sustainable outcomes from the land, whose responsibility is it, the tenant or the owner? These are all considerations we must make if we are going to pass along our land ethic for future generations. The idea of a sustainable future includes passing a deep faith, thanks, and worship of our Lord Jesus Christ. The Father created this land, and our responsibility is to care for the soil and our soul and pass that knowledge to the next generation.

> [4] **Jesus answered: "Watch out that no one deceives you.** [5] *For many will come in my name, claiming, 'I am the Messiah,' and will deceive many.* [6] *You will hear of wars and rumors of wars, but see to it that you are not alarmed. Such things must happen, but the end is still to come.* [7] *Nation will rise against nation, and kingdom against kingdom. There will be famines and earthquakes in various places.* [8] *All these are the beginning of birth pains.*
>
> [9] *"Then you will be handed over to be persecuted and put to death, and you will be hated by all nations because of me.* [10] *At that time many will turn away from the faith and will betray and hate each other,* [11] *and many false prophets will appear and deceive many people.* [12] *Because of the increase of wickedness, the love of most will grow cold,* [13] *but the one who stands firm to the end will be saved.* [14] *And this gospel of the kingdom will be preached in the whole world as a testimony to all nations, and then the end will come.*

The Bible describes the end times rather vividly. Jesus's own words foretold of a very unpleasant and trying time before He returns to this earth before it is restored to its Eden-like nature. It is a time of worldwide pestilence, famine, and drought. He tells us that we must hold firm during this period to the true faith in Him. The life of a follower of Christ will be difficult, and many will fall away in order to keep their lives comfortable. We do not know when this will occur, but so much of the news today seems to be indicative of such times. Especially when it comes to the events brought about in this new reality of COVID-19, and the resulting political discord of how to deal with its effects, it seems humanity is being challenged in ways that are very real yet surreal at the same time. This is a time to stop…reflect on what is important and recognize Christ as our savior. It is a time to repent of our sin and begin living in a manner reflective of our Christian beliefs. Can other people see clearly that you are a Christian, or are you going into hiding to protect your comfortable lifestyle? It seems more and more of our freedoms are being challenged—in the name of protecting public safety. Are we trying to save ourselves, or are we willing to hand the situation to Christ and boldly proclaim His power over every aspect of our lives? It is time to make some tough decisions. Again, from Matthew 24:

[45] *"Who then is the faithful and wise servant, whom the master has put in charge of the servants in his household to give them their food at the proper time?* [46] *It will be good for that servant whose master finds him doing so when he returns.* [47] *Truly I tell you, he will put him in charge of all his possessions.* [48] *But suppose that servant is wicked and says to himself, 'My master is staying away a long time,'* [49] *and he then begins to beat his fellow servants and to eat and drink with drunkards.* [50] *The master of that servant will come on a day when he does not expect him and at an hour he is not aware of.* [51] *He will cut him to pieces and assign him a place with the hypocrites, where there will be weeping and gnashing of teeth.*

I believe Jesus uses these statements to get us to think about how we will live our life, even though it may seem like God is far away, or not having an impact on our daily lives. As caretakers of His creation, we have a responsibility to produce healthy and nutritious food for the people of the world. Is this your attitude as to what you are doing as you manage your farm? Feeding others is one of the most noble occupations one can undertake. The end times are getting closer, and the world is going to need genuine, devoted, Christian farmers to produce food during these trying times. Are you up to the task? Are you utilizing your land to the best of its capability to produce food? With healthy soil, and healthy soul, the land will be being utilized to its most sustainable capability. That will be the best we can do on this earth and the outcome will be in God's hands, to His glory.

24

The Wise and Faithful Servant

So, what are God's instructions for us as we wait for Jesus's return to Judge the world? Will He find us using wise management and faithful worship demonstrated through how we farm? Will he find farmers that love their neighbor and are genuinely concerned about making sure others are fed and cared for, rather than being caught up in our own security and comforts? Jesus gave us the instructions for living in this world under God's grace. He tells us exactly the type of people he wants us to be. He is looking for those who are willing to absorb and reflect His light upon the world and be the "good soil, bringing in the harvest—a hundredfold." How we utilize His light—grace—is how he will know us. A good tree, with good roots, produces good fruit. Jesus clearly states our purpose in this life in the Book of John:

15 "I am the true vine, and my Father is the gardener. 2 He cuts off every branch in me that bears no fruit, while every branch that does bear fruit he prunes[a] so that it will be even more fruitful. ³ You are already clean because of the word I have spoken to you. ⁴ Remain in me, as I also remain in you. No branch can bear fruit by itself; it must remain in the vine. Neither can you bear fruit unless you remain in me.

⁵ "I am the vine; you are the branches. If you remain in me and I in you, you will bear much fruit; apart from me you can do nothing. ⁶ If you do not remain in me, you are like a branch that is thrown away and withers; such branches are picked up, thrown into the fire and burned. ⁷ If you remain in me and my words remain in you, ask whatever you wish, and it will be done for you. ⁸ This is to my Father's glory, that you bear much fruit, showing yourselves to be my disciples.

⁹ "As the Father has loved me, so have I loved you. Now remain in my love. ¹⁰ If you keep my commands, you will remain in my love, just as I have kept my Father's commands and remain in his love. ¹¹ I have told you this so that my joy may be in you and that your joy may be complete. ¹² My command is this: Love each other as I have loved you. ¹³ Greater love has no one than this: to lay down one's life for one's friends. ¹⁴ You are my friends if you do what I command. ¹⁵ I no longer call you servants, because a servant does not know his master's business. Instead, I have called you friends, for everything that I learned from my Father I have made known to you. ¹⁶ You did not choose me, but I chose you and appointed you so that you might go and bear fruit—fruit that will last—and so that whatever you ask in my name the Father will give you. ¹⁷ This is my command: Love each other.

Jesus died and rose again to forgive our sin and regenerate our relationship with our creator. He took our sin upon himself so that our souls can return to our creator—who loves us—pure and blameless. He did this to reconcile the whole world from its sinful condition, and it has been done. It is finished. We wait for His return. In the meantime, our job is to share this good news with others. The best way to do this is to love each other. Just as Jesus fed the five thousand because they were hungry, so you, too, can feed the hungry—at least a hundredfold. Again, Luke 18:

8 Still other seed fell on good soil. It came up and yielded a crop, a hundred times more than was sown."

When he said this, he called out, "Whoever has ears to hear, let them hear."

Do you have ears?

So now what? If you have ears, what do you do now? Listen to these words in 2nd Corinthians 13:

5 Examine yourselves to see whether you are in the faith; test yourselves. Do you not realize that Christ Jesus is in you—unless, of course, you fail the test? 6 And I trust that you will discover that we have not failed the test. 7 Now we pray to God that you will not do anything wrong—not so that people will see that we have stood the test but so that you will do what is right even though we may seem to have failed. 8 For we cannot do anything against the truth, but only for the truth. 9 We are glad whenever we are weak but you are strong; and our prayer is that you may be fully restored. 10 This is why I write these things when I am absent, that when I come I may not have to be harsh in my use of authority—the authority the Lord gave me for building you up, not for tearing you down

11 Finally, brothers and sisters, rejoice! Strive for full restoration, encourage one another, be of one mind, live in peace. And the God of love and peace will be with you.

And in Hebrews 10:

23 Let us hold unswervingly to the hope we profess, for he who promised is faithful. 24 And let us consider how we may spur one

another on toward love and good deeds, [25] not giving up meeting together, as some are in the habit of doing, but encouraging one another—and all the more as you see the Day approaching.

To live like you have ears is to hear and live the words of Christ. First of all, you must recognize His creation and provision for you. We are to accept His invitation and submit to His care. Secondly, we need to respond to His words, and take them seriously. By submitting our life to Him, we will act according to His truth. Lastly, we do His will and thank Him, grateful for His care. This will provide the sustainable peace which passes all understanding. Accept His grace, and then, being good soil, produce a rich harvest sharing the light we receive from Him with others.

25

Truth

Pontius Pilate asked Jesus, "What is Truth?" Jesus said nothing. What could He say? The whole truth and nothing but the truth was standing right in front of him, and Pilate could not see it. If you know the biblical account, Pilate tried every way possible to release Jesus. Even his wife cautioned him, "Have nothing to do with this man," yet Pilate could not seem to get rid of him or ignore the Man. It was his job to keep the peace between the many different political and religious powers of the day and implement justice amongst the people. Think of it. Pilate was in a no-win situation. No matter how he ruled, a large portion of the populous was going to be upset. The Jewish hierarchy wanted Jesus dead. The Roman government wanted peace and tolerance, so long as you pay your taxes. The fledgling Christians were helpless and hiding. No one came to Jesus's defense, and the biggest event in the history of the world played out. It was almost as if the event was fully planned out and the outcome predetermined. It was. That is the truth. We read in John 3, beginning with the famous verse 16:

¹⁶ For God so loved the world that he gave his one and only Son, that whoever believes in him shall not perish but have eternal life. ¹⁷ For God did not send his Son into the world to condemn the world, but to save the world through him. ¹⁸ Whoever believes in him is not condemned, but whoever does not believe stands condemned already because they have not believed in the name of God's one and only Son. ¹⁹ This is the verdict: Light has come into the world, but people loved darkness instead of light because their deeds were evil. ²⁰ Everyone who does evil hates the light, and will not come into the light for fear that their deeds will be exposed. ²¹ But whoever lives by the truth comes into the light, so that it may be seen plainly that what they have done has been done in the sight of God.

Think of these words of Christ, in context of what is going on today. We are choosing various beliefs about world events—all of which are nothing but a distraction from the Truth. If you have read the Bible, you know that this is also pre-destined. At the end times, we will not be able to tell the difference between right and wrong. Families will disagree and be split. Read in Revelation the situation that the seven churches will be in toward the end. Political unrest, with deeply divided core beliefs. What about Covid-19 and all its variants? How should we deal with it? Vaccinate or not?

What about how we produce our food? Are highly efficient feedlots the most sustainable method? Is hydroponics going to provide the safest and most sustainable method to provide food? Is GMO technology safe? Are the chemicals we apply on our crops safe? What about antibiotics in animals? What about global warming—is it real or simply just a mechanism to control and tax our lives? Is social justice or critical race theory Christian-based ideology? Is the world fair? Will science provide the best way to ensure that world resources are equitably moved and provided across the planet? Where will we place our faith?

I have news for you. The Truth is the same today, just as it was at creation, and just as it was at Pilate's time. The Truth is, you are going to die—no matter what you believe about any of today's controversies. No matter what you believe about how we should manage our actions or develop public policy around our core beliefs, none of it matters unless you approach it with this core belief: God is in charge. He always has been. He sent His Son for your salvation. That is the Truth.

So, no matter how you choose to farm, none of it will matter unless it is done to God's glory. He gave us a system of life—through the free availability of light. It is given in the physical world as sunlight and is freely available for you—just as the grace of God is given to you through the death and resurrection of Jesus Christ. It is time for you to choose how you wish to use this free resource—not only to improve your soil health, but for the health of your own soul. Fill your soul with light—and become the "good soil" using your ears to hear, to provide the good harvest that only Jesus—The Truth—can provide. Amen.

Book 2

"Heal Their Land"
1

In the book I wrote titled *Farmers of Light*, I made the case that the Bible has so very much to say about how our souls can be kept healthy by using God's principles. Jesus often used agriculture and discussions about planting seeds and plant growth, to explain what it takes to produce a useful harvest. Jesus would say, "Do you have ears?" This statement is always a call for you to think more deeply into what he was saying, usually in the form of a parable, to illustrate a very simple and visible physical process that also parallels a spiritual truth. He used these parables so that we could relate them to something we could easily see and understand, and then use that to comprehend the nature of God and His plan for our salvation. This is the truth in its purest form. John 3:

> *16 For God so loved the world that he gave his one and only Son, that whoever believes in him shall not perish but have eternal life.*

The purpose of this book is to take a much deeper look into how management of our souls compares to the health of our environment and how God's creation and his systems provide for us everything we need if we just simply depend on and trust in him as he has promised us. It requires us to take leap of faith toward him—not to the most recent scientific journals, internet news, or carbon-sequestration schemes to provide direction in our lives. Taking care of his creation is our job. We are his creation, and we have been instructed to care for his garden. God said at the end of every day of creation that "It was good." And after day six, the day he created man he said, "It was very good." What has changed? Well, of course, Satan deceived man, and as a result, man thought he could do whatever he wanted, and sin entered the world. Satan's greatest lie is that he has fooled man into thinking that since man caused all the problems in the world, that man can fix them. Where is God in that discussion? Satan's has tricked man into thinking that he can save himself. Ever since sin entered the world, man has been trying to save himself. This will be a fruitless effort.

Today, we are talking about climate change, floods, droughts, extremes, warming, cooling, greenhouse gas emissions, cow farts, plant-based proteins, genetically modified plants and organisms, cover crops, carbon exchanges, biofuels, carbon dioxide capture, land use change, hydroponics, vertical farming, solar technologies, electric cars, remote-sensing technology, policy making, carbon economies, incentives to change. Take your pick. What must we do to save the world? What are you going to do on your farm to make sure you are not contributing? What are you going to choose to buy and what are you going to consume to do your part? What are you doing to do to heal the planet? Are you working on offsetting your own carbon footprint? You know…if we don't get started on this, the world is going to self-destruct!

My question is, where is God in this discussion? Didn't he create it all? Do you think he does not know how to save it? Just who do we think we are? The book of Job speaks very directly to this issue. Job had it all.

God allowed Satan to take it away, just to teach us all how we need to conduct ourselves no matter our circumstances. God very bluntly tells Job the truth:

³⁸ Then the LORD spoke to Job out of the storm. He said:
²"Who is this that obscures my plans
with words without knowledge?
³ Brace yourself like a man;
I will question you,
and you shall answer me.
⁴"Where were you when I laid the earth's foundation?
Tell me, if you understand.
⁵ Who marked off its dimensions? Surely you know!
Who stretched a measuring line across it?
⁶ On what were its footings set,
or who laid its cornerstone—
⁷ while the morning stars sang together
and all the angels shouted for joy?
⁸ "Who shut up the sea behind doors
when it burst forth from the womb,
⁹ when I made the clouds its garment
and wrapped it in thick darkness,
¹⁰ when I fixed limits for it
and set its doors and bars in place,
¹¹ when I said, 'This far you may come and no farther;
here is where your proud waves halt'?
¹² "Have you ever given orders to the morning,
or shown the dawn its place,
¹³ that it might take the earth by the edges
and shake the wicked out of it?
¹⁴ The earth takes shape like clay under a seal;
its features stand out like those of a garment.

¹⁵ The wicked are denied their light,
and their upraised arm is broken.
¹⁶ "Have you journeyed to the springs of the sea
or walked in the recesses of the deep?
¹⁷ Have the gates of death been shown to you?
Have you seen the gates of the deepest darkness?
¹⁸ Have you comprehended the vast expanses of the earth?
Tell me, if you know all this.
¹⁹ "What is the way to the abode of light?
And where does darkness reside?
²⁰ Can you take them to their places?
Do you know the paths to their dwellings?
²¹ Surely you know, for you were already born!
You have lived so many years!
²² "Have you entered the storehouses of the snow
or seen the storehouses of the hail,
²³ which I reserve for times of trouble,
for days of war and battle?
²⁴ What is the way to the place where the lightning is dispersed,
or the place where the east winds are scattered over the earth?
²⁵ Who cuts a channel for the torrents of rain,
and a path for the thunderstorm,
²⁶ to water a land where no one lives,
an uninhabited desert,
²⁷ to satisfy a desolate wasteland
and make it sprout with grass?
²⁸ Does the rain have a father?
Who fathers the drops of dew?
²⁹ From whose womb comes the ice?
Who gives birth to the frost from the heavens
³⁰ when the waters become hard as stone,
when the surface of the deep is frozen?

[31] "Can you bind the chains of the Pleiades?
Can you loosen Orion's belt?
[32] Can you bring forth the constellations in their seasons
or lead out the Bear with its cubs?
[33] Do you know the laws of the heavens?
Can you set up God's dominion over the earth?
[34] "Can you raise your voice to the clouds
and cover yourself with a flood of water?
[35] Do you send the lightning bolts on their way?
Do they report to you, 'Here we are'?
[36] Who gives the ibis wisdom
or gives the rooster understanding?
[37] Who has the wisdom to count the clouds?
Who can tip over the water jars of the heavens
[38] when the dust becomes hard
and the clods of earth stick together?
[39] "Do you hunt the prey for the lioness
and satisfy the hunger of the lions
[40] when they crouch in their dens
or lie in wait in a thicket?
[41] Who provides food for the raven
when its young cry out to God
and wander about for lack of food?

God is saying, "Job, Listen up. Just who do you think you are?" God is saying the same thing to us. We feel sorry for Job, at least I do. But when we decide to question God and think we can figure out how to save ourselves, we really are in no better shape than Job! The good news is that God had Job's back the whole time. Job recovered all that he had lost and wound up with even more.

Is it any wonder that this planet is in the condition it is in? Why would we expect anything different? If we are going to save ourselves, do you suppose God might just say, "Okay…Go for it. See how far you can get." We have the privilege from God to exercise our free will. But free will is what allows us to choose whether we will follow him or go our own way. It is up to us. God has given us very clear instructions as to how to keep our land healthy, but "Do we have ears?" Are we listening…? Do we have the frame of mind to receive? Are we able to receive and produce, like healthy soil?

2

Jesus's question, "Do you have ears?" is given to us to consider his words and self-reflect upon what he was saying. Yes, we have ears. What are ears for? Listening. But listening without context, or a deeper understanding or consideration of what we are hearing is likely quickly forgotten and is mostly just noise. On the other hand, truly thinking and listening to what we hear, and giving it consideration, is how the Holy Spirit works in our lives. St. Paul writes in his letter to the Romans:

[16] But not all the Israelites accepted the good news. For Isaiah says, "Lord, who has believed our message?"[h] [17] Consequently, faith comes from hearing the message, and the message is heard through the word about Christ. [18] But I ask: Did they not hear? Of course they did: "Their voice has gone out into all the earth, their words to the ends of the world."

[19] Again I ask: Did Israel not understand? First, Moses says,
"I will make you envious by those who are not a nation;
I will make you angry by a nation that has no understanding."

²⁰ And Isaiah boldly says,
"I was found by those who did not seek me; I revealed myself to
those who did not ask for me."
²¹ But concerning Israel he says,
"All day long I have held out my hands
to a disobedient and obstinate people."

What are ears for? Hearing the Word of God is how we receive faith. If we simply tune out his word or tell ourselves—*that won't work here*, or *I tried that before*, or *I can't because*…are we really listening with our ears, or we are we tuning out and rejecting before we have even listened? Why might we want to listen? 2 Timothy 3:

¹⁶ All Scripture is God-breathed and is useful for teaching, rebuking, correcting and training in righteousness, ¹⁷ so that the servant of God[a] may be thoroughly equipped for every good work.

God's word is given to us for our own benefit. Tuning it out, ignoring it, or just simply rejecting it is to deny ourselves an opportunity to grow in faith. It is a denial of the creator, and a rejection of his grace for you. That is why Jesus ask us if we have ears. He wants us to hear what he is saying and trust that what he has said is the truth.

I made the observation in *"Farmers of Light"* that the health of our souls and the health of our soils are very similar. It takes a principled and intentional approach to manage our lives and God's creation to his glory. He gives us those principles in his Word. By listening to his Word, we can obtain insight as to how his creation really works. He created it all; He knows how it works. Our job is to listen to his Word and produce a useful harvest—good fruit.

So, what happens if we have not followed the principles? Our soils will not function to their full potential. Many years of consecutive mismanagement can have devastating effects. Soils will lose organic matter—

carbon. In pursuit of maximizing our yields to our own benefit, rather than to God's glory, in line with his principles…have we been trying to save ourselves? Where will the good fruit come from after we have destroyed the ability of the soil to produce? This is to our own demise. Yet we need to produce yield to remain on the land. How do we do this? If we are losing organic matter, losing carbon…we are losing potential. How do we heal the land?

We must recognize that our management—by our own choosing—has quite possibly not been in line with the soil health principles. This puts things into context. We see that what we have been doing is not working and is not sustainable. We know we must change. This is an "Ah-ha!" moment. This is what it means to have ears. Understanding your context is now being recognized as a new soil health principle. "Know your context." Recognition of the need for change is the very first step in your soil health journey. Now the question is, how do I change? Where do I start?

The Bible has perfect instructions. God makes a promise to King Solomon—the wisest man that ever lived. 2 Chronicles:

If my people, who are called by my name, will humble themselves and pray and seek my face and turn from their wicked ways, then I will hear from heaven, and I will forgive their sin and will heal their land.

Admitting our mistakes and desiring to do better are where we start. This is true for our soul, and our soil. We are made from dust. Turning dust into soil takes some work. It begins by humbling ourselves and asking the Lord for help. He promises to hear us and provide healing…both for the land and our soul. This is how regeneration works. Healing our land is God's work… on our behalf. Attempting to heal our land without God's help is like attempting to save ourselves…Good luck!

3

Two hundred years after King Solomon received this great promise—to heal the land—God chose a very reluctant Jeremiah to be a prophet to the people of Judah. His job was to tell the people that because they had forgotten who God was, an invading army was going to wipe most of them out. Not only that but he was also telling the King that he will need to surrender if they are to survive. Imagine that. Jeremiah did not want the job. Who would? Nevertheless, Thy will be done, and Jeremiah voiced to the people some of the harshest yet eloquent verses in the Bible. What he wrote was full of warning and promise, danger and hope, law and gospel. But throughout the book, which is worth sitting down and reading in its entirety given today's circumstances, Jeremiah warns the people to repent of their worship of false gods and return to God the creator. They thought they knew how to save themselves, but if they continued down that path, the outcome would not be good. Jeremiah 5:

Declare this in the house of Jacob and proclaim it in Judah:
21"Hear this,
O foolish and senseless people,

who have eyes but do not see,
who have ears but do not hear.
²²Do you not fear Me?"
declares the LORD.

God asks if the people have ears. Do we have ears? Are we today able to hear what God is telling us? God gave clear instructions and fair warning. Jeremiah 17:

This is what the LORD says:
"Cursed is the man who trusts in mankind,
who makes the flesh his strength
and turns his heart from the LORD.
⁶He will be like a shrub in the desert;
he will not see when prosperity comes.
He will dwell in the parched places of the desert,
in a salt land where no one lives.
⁷But blessed is the man who trusts in the LORD,
whose confidence is in Him.
⁸He is like a tree planted by the waters
that sends out its roots toward the stream.
It does not fear when the heat comes,
and its leaves are always green.
It does not worry in a year of drought,
nor does it cease to produce fruit.

When we trust in our own solutions to problems rather than trust that God has things under control, aren't we just really worrying about ourselves and our own well-being? There will not likely be any sustainable outcomes or positive results from those efforts. On the other hand, trusting in the Lord will give us the peace of mind and confidence that will produce positive results—fruit. I hope you would rather live by the stream, instead of in the desert. We have the choice.

4

Healing the Land is God's promise. We are placed into this world to manage our souls and soils for him, but know this: the only healing we truly need has already occurred on our behalf! The promise has already been fulfilled! This is the truth of the Gospel! The pathway to regeneration of our souls is wide open. Christ's death and resurrection has already defeated sin, death, and the power of the devil. Choosing to believe it and remain on this path is to fulfill God's desire for your life. Along the path will be many thorns and thistles, but finding your way through is to follow Christ—who is leading the way, by His light.

A fully healed land is not going to be truly recognized until Christ returns in his full glory to fully restore its Eden-like nature. In the meantime, we are to care for what we have been given to shine as an example to others so they can get a glimpse of what that might look like. We are in the end times. We have been since Christ was crucified to take on all our sin. He is risen! We do not know when he will return. In the meantime, our job is to produce fruit that is to God's glory to build his kingdom.

Carbon is an indicator of soil health. Faith is an indicator of soul health. Just as we can stick a tiling spade into our soil to look for indicators of soil health, God has a tiling spade and can easily look into your soul to see how you are doing in soul management. He is looking for souls that can produce an outcome to his glory…soils that can produce a bountiful harvest. It is not something you can obtain through quick fixes and silver bullets. It takes some learning and willingness to hear…listening and then acting. It also takes discernment, to know when not to bite off more than you can chew. It is a journey. Nobody has ever lived it perfectly, other than Jesus Christ. Do not get depressed about your context. Use it to begin your journey. Ask Jesus to guide your steps and lead you down the path. Be open-minded. Use the resources you have. Do not be afraid of making some investments that can help improve your management toward soil health—but think them through. Have a vision of how you want your soils to function and think about whether the decisions you make today are taking you toward those goals. Do not be afraid to ask for help. Others have been where you are, and others are where you want to be. But most importantly, remember that we are God's creation, His garden, His soil. He knew you before you were born, and we are his children. He wants to help you, regenerate your soul, and bring you home.

We are entering uncertain times economically, politically, physically, and environmentally. One thing is certain, however, and it has been true since the fall of man. Sustenance of life on this planet is fully dependent upon God our Father and creator. He gives us what we need to support each other, through the production of food from His creation. How we manage those gifts and understanding how to best use them is up to us, with His guiding hand. The world needs, and always has needed, God-fearing farmers and ranchers to manage and conduct this work. This country is going to need every one of you—those who have ears—to produce healthy produce for the people of this earth to His glory. Isaiah 8:

8 Then I heard the voice of the Lord saying, "Whom shall I send?
And who will go for us"
And I said, "Here am I. Send me!"

And finally, James 3:18

And the seed whose fruit is righteousness is sown in peace by those who make peace.

Dear Father in Heaven, we pray for you to open our ears, to hear your word, and use it to help guide us on our regenerative journey, to Your glory. Help us, encourage us, connect us with others, and provide wisdom and discernment as we travel this path together. Help us to recognize and fulfill our responsibility to tend your garden. Most of all, we thank you for the true regenerative nature given to us through Your son, Jesus. We pray in His Name, Amen.